EAT SMART

**The Random House Guide
to Diet and Nutrition**

Random House
New York

Prepared by the editors of Random House, Inc., in cooperation with Sachem Publishing Associates, Inc.

Library of Congress Cataloging in Publication Data

Main entry under title:
Eat smart.
  1. Reducing diets. I. Random House (Firm)
RM222.2.E23 1984   613.2   84-3406

ISBN 0-394-53445-X

Preface

The relationship between good health and individual eating habits continues to be one of the most important and interesting subjects in modern everyday life. More and more people want to know how to choose nutritionally sound foods, control their weight while maintaining good nutrition and energy levels, and adjust their diets to meet certain physical or metabolic needs. It is for this readership that the guidelines, meal plans, special diets, and calorie and nutrition tables of *Eat Smart* have been prepared.

We would like to thank all who helped to produce *Eat Smart*. The expert advice and contributions of Joan Tarduogno Roberts, R.D., M.M.Sc., Clinical Nutrition Specialist at Yale— New Haven Hospital, New Haven, Connecticut, were invaluable. As adviser to the book, Ms. Roberts readily shared her expertise in nutrition, particularly in planning the Basic Healthy Diet and the section Basic Weight Loss.

Special thanks go also to Susan Carter Elliott and Joyce O'Connor, for editing; Carlo De Lucia, for design; Carolyn Westberg, Keith Hollaman, Susan Israel, and Judy Bouck Porter, for editorial assistance; and Patricia W. Ehresmann, for production management.

Contents

6

A Word About Nutrition, Health, and Diet

The importance of proper nutrition is universally recognized. Almost daily, new discoveries are made about the effect of some dietary ingredient on health. In recent years, for example, the incidence of many serious or life-threatening diseases—including heart disease, high blood pressure, diabetes, and some types of cancer—has been linked to eating habits. Even life expectancy is thought to be affected by nutrition. A few short years ago the average person knew little about nutrition and probably seldom thought about it. Today, nearly everyone has some degree of interest in the subject. The quest for health and vitality has prompted many people to improve their diets, increase their activity levels, and regulate their weight.

Nutritional needs are like fingerprints; no two are alike. It is impossible to develop a diet that is perfectly balanced for every individual because individual needs are influenced by a number of factors: age, sex, body size, general state of health, activity level, climate, and metabolism, to name just a few. The purpose of *Eat Smart,* the Random House guide to diet and nutrition, is to offer some general guidelines for formulating a diet that is nutritionally sound for most healthy people, and to suggest ways to meet special needs associated with certain health problems.

This book describes the fundamentals of an average healthy diet and offers a seven-day meal plan for sensible eating. This same meal plan is also adjusted for a basic weight-loss program of 1800 or 1200 calories per day. In addition, there are outlines for diets that reduce the intake of sodium, cholesterol, carbohydrates, and purine and for diets that increase the intake

A Word About Nutrition, Health, and Diet

of fiber, protein, and potassium. Suggestions for combining complementary proteins enhance the vegetarian diet. Also described are the liquid, bland, and low-residue diets sometimes prescribed for certain illnesses, as well as the features of the diabetic diet.

The diets are supplemented by lists and charts covering food groups, the food sources of vitamins and minerals, the recommended daily allowances for vitamins and minerals, height and weight standards, and the composition of foods. The table Composition of Foods covers more than a thousand separate foods, listing the key nutritional data for an average serving portion of each: calories, protein, fat, carbohydrates (total and fiber), and sodium. This breakdown of the nutritional values will allow you to evaluate individual foods and develop meal plans based on the guidelines offered in each specific diet.

No sustained change in eating habits should be undertaken without consulting your physician. Certain regimens contained in this book, such as the liquid, bland, low-purine, diabetic, high-potassium, and low-residue diets, should not be followed unless prescribed by a physician, as they are designed for use only when specific physiological or disease conditions are present.

Basic Healthy Diet

Long-held ideas about what constitutes a healthy diet have recently been re-examined, and a number of new discoveries have come to light. The exact make-up of a properly balanced diet is different for each person, depending on age, sex, body size, health, and activity level. Yet the fundamentals of a sensible eating program apply to all of us, regardless of our individual needs.

Variety and moderation are important rules. About 40 different components—including vitamins and minerals (see page 16), amino acids (from proteins), fatty acids (from animal fats and vegetable oils), and calories supplied by proteins, fats, and carbohydrates—are needed to maintain normal bodily health. Since no single food will provide all of these together, a number of foods must be eaten every day. These foods should include selections from the basic food groups; namely, fruits and vegetables, breads and cereals, dairy products, and meats (see page 14). But the foods chosen from each of the groups should also be varied, since every food has a slightly different nutritional profile. Too much of a single nutrient does not offer any particular benefits, and overconsumption of one food often means that other foods are being neglected in the diet.

It is important to avoid foods that contain too much saturated fat and cholesterol, for these substances may contribute to heart disease and cancer. It is not necessary to eat much meat. Poultry and fish are preferable to beef, pork, and lamb. Choose lean meat and cut off any excess fat. Limit organ meats. Eat no more than three eggs a week and reduce the amounts of cream, butter, shortening, and hydrogenated margarine. Use low-fat dairy products.

When fats and cholesterol are reduced, so are the calories normally supplied by these nutrients. Those who do not wish to lose weight will need to replace the lost calories. Carbohydrates, which contain approximately half the calories of fats, are an ideal substitute. Complex carbohydrates—such as legumes, fruits, vegetables, and whole-grain and cereal products—which provide nutrients, fiber, and a feeling of fullness, are preferable to simple carbohydrates—such as refined flour and sugars—which supply calories and not much else. Complex carbohydrates should be increased and eaten in combination to supply complete protein (see Complementary Proteins, page 45).

Sugar, sodium, and alcohol should be consumed only in moderate amounts. Excess sugar contributes to tooth decay and may aggravate other health problems. High levels of sodium—primarily from table salt but also from snack foods, pickled and processed foods, baking soda and powder, MSG (monosodium glutamate, a flavor enhancer), and certain medications—are a factor in the development of high blood pressure. Alcohol, high in calories and low in nutrients, has been implicated in birth defects, cancer, and liver disease when used excessively.

The following seven-day menu plan provides a healthy diet with a balance of nutrients to meet the needs of most people. Choose portion sizes that will allow you to maintain your ideal weight. The menu plan can be used as a guide to the development of additional meal plans that reflect personal and family preferences.

7-DAY MENU PLAN—Basic Healthy Diet*

SUNDAY

Breakfast

½ grapefruit
scrambled egg
whole-wheat bagel
margarine
skim milk

Lunch

marinated vegetable
  and cheese plate
whole-wheat roll
pear

Dinner

fresh pork roast
applesauce
new potatoes boiled in skin
three-bean salad
ice cream

MONDAY

Breakfast

orange juice
oatmeal with honey
fruit yogurt

Lunch

vegetable soup
peanut butter sand-
  wich on whole-
  wheat bread
skim milk
apple

Dinner

roast chicken
bread stuffing
carrot and raisin salad
steamed broccoli
margarine
tapioca pudding

---

* All margarine is from corn oil; all oil is corn oil.

7-DAY MENU PLAN—Basic Healthy Diet

TUESDAY

Breakfast

orange sections
granola cereal
skim milk

Lunch

fruit salad
chicken salad sand-
   wich on whole-wheat
   bread
oatmeal cookies

Dinner

black beans and yellow rice with hot sauce
tossed salad
black bread

WEDNESDAY

Breakfast

grapefruit juice
soft-cooked egg
whole-wheat toast
margarine

Lunch

turkey sandwich on
   pumpernickel bread
skim milk
chocolate-chip cookies

Dinner

veal scallopini
steamed green beans with almonds
French bread

7-DAY MENU PLAN—Basic Healthy Diet

THURSDAY

Breakfast	Lunch

orange juice
bran muffins with peanut
  butter
	chef salad with oil
	  and vinegar
	whole-wheat roll
	grapes

Dinner

beef stew with noodles
tomato salad
watermelon

FRIDAY

Breakfast	Lunch
bran cereal banana skim milk	cheese, tomato, and lettuce sandwich on pita bread

Dinner

baked halibut
brown rice
zucchini salad with yogurt dressing
baked custard

7-DAY MENU PLAN—Basic Healthy Diet

SATURDAY

Breakfast

orange and grapefruit
   sections
whole-wheat pancakes
syrup
skim milk

Lunch

grape juice
tuna salad on whole-
   wheat bread

Dinner

pasta with tomato sauce
meatballs
green salad

Food Groups

One way to assure a well-balanced diet is to select foods every day from each of the major food groups. The greater the variety, the less likely you are to develop a deficiency in or an excess of any single nutrient. Each food group provides some of the 40 essential nutrients.

Food	Suggested Daily Amounts

Milk Products

1 cup skim milk; 1 cup yogurt; 1 oz. cheese; ½ cup ice cream	2–4 servings in any combination

Meat

3–4 oz. meat, poultry, fish; 2 tbs. peanut butter; ½–1 cup legumes	2 or more servings in any combination

Fruits and Vegetables

½–1 cup any vegetable or fruit (or equivalent, as 1 med. apple, orange, etc.)	4 or more servings including one source of vitamin C and, every other day, a green or yellow vegetable

Breads and Cereals

1 slice bread; ½ cup rice; 1 cup pasta; ½ cup cereal	4 or more servings in any combination

Fats and Sweets

butter; margarine; salad dressing; sugar	none required

Recommended Daily Dietary Allowances

(Source: National Research Council)

	Adult Male	Adult Female
Vitamin A	5000 IU	4000 IU
Vitamin B₁ (thiamine)	1.2–1.4 mg	1.0 mg
Vitamin B₂ (riboflavin)	1.4–1.6 mg	1.2 mg
Vitamin B₃ (niacin)	16–18 mg	13 mg
Vitamin B₆ (pyridoxine)	2.2 mg	2.0 mg
Vitamin B₁₂ (cobalamin or cyanoco-balamin)	3 mcg	3 mcg
Pantothenic Acid	none established	
Biotin	none established	
Folic Acid	400 mcg	400 mcg
Vitamin C (ascorbic acid)	60 mg	60 mg
Vitamin D	200 IU	200 IU
Vitamin E	15 IU	12 IU
Vitamin K	none established	
Calcium	800 mcg	800 mg
Copper	none established	
Fluorine	none established	
Iodine	150 mcg	150 mcg
Iron	10 mg	10–18 mg
Magnesium	350 mg	300 mg
Phosphorus	800 mg	800 mg
Potassium	none established	
Zinc	15 mg	15 mg

Vitamins and Minerals

The following lists indicate those foods that are high in specific vitamins and minerals. A balanced diet, such as the Basic Healthy Diet (pages 8–13), should provide sufficient amounts of vitamins and minerals.

VITAMINS

Vitamin A
Beneficial to: vision, reproduction, growth; mucous membranes, bones, skin, hair, teeth, gums

> butter, margarine
> cheese (whole milk)
> eggs
> fruits, especially apricots, cantaloupe, cherries, mangoes, papaya, peaches, persimmons, watermelon
> kidney
> liver
> milk (whole)
> vegetables (dark green and deep yellow), especially broccoli, cabbage, carrots, chard, collards, corn, cress, kale, pumpkin, spinach, winter squash

Vitamin B$_1$ (thiamine)
Beneficial to: growth, digestion, appetite, metabolism of carbohydrates; nervous system, muscles, heart

> cereals (whole grain)
> crab
> eggs
> lima beans
> meats, especially ham; heart, kidney, liver
> raisins
> rice (brown)
> soybeans
> sunflower seeds

Vitamins and Minerals

    vegetables, especially asparagus, green
      beans, green peas
    yeast (brewer's, debittered)

Vitamin B$_2$ (riboflavin)
*Beneficial to: respiration, vision, growth,
reproduction, metabolism of protein,
carbohydrates, and fats; skin, nails, hair, lips,
tongue*
    cereals (whole grain)
    eggs (raw)
    fish
    lima beans
    meats, especially beef, ham; heart, kidney,
      liver
    milk
    poultry, especially chicken
    sunflower seeds
    vegetables (dark green and leafy), especially
      broccoli, green peas, kale, spinach
    yeast (brewer's, debittered)

Vitamin B$_3$ (niacin)
*Beneficial to: circulation, digestion, growth,
metabolism of carbohydrates; skin*
    cereals (whole grain)
    eggs
    fish, especially tuna
    meats, especially ham, rabbit; heart, liver,
      kidney
    nuts, sunflower seeds
    peas (green)
    poultry, especially chicken, turkey
    soybeans
    yeast (brewer's, debittered)

Vitamin B$_6$ (pyridoxine)
*Beneficial to: metabolism of protein,
carbohydrates, and fats; hormones, nervous
system, red blood cells, skin*
    bananas

Vitamins and Minerals

cereals (whole grain)
chicken
egg yolks
fish, especially salmon, tuna
legumes, especially white beans, soybeans
meats, especially kidney, liver
nuts, especially walnuts, filberts
peanuts
potatoes
prunes, raisins
rice (brown)
shellfish
sunflower seeds
sweet potatoes
vegetables (dark green and leafy)
wheat germ
yeast (brewer's, debittered)

Vitamin B_{12} (cobalamin or cyanocobalamin)—found only in foods of animal origin
Beneficial to: growth, digestion, metabolism of protein, carbohydrates, and fats; bone marrow, red blood cells, nervous system
cheese
eggs
fish, especially herring, sardines
meat and meat by-products, especially beef;
    heart, kidney, liver
milk
shellfish, especially clams, crabs, oysters

Pantothenic Acid—in most foods
Beneficial to: digestion, metabolism of carbohydrates and fats; skin, immune system, glands
cereals (whole grain)
eggs
legumes, especially peas, soybeans
lobster
meat, especially heart, kidney, liver
peanuts

sesame flour
sunflower seeds
vegetables
yeast (brewer's, debittered)

Biotin—in most foods
Beneficial to: circulation, growth, metabolism of protein, carbohydrates, and fats; hair, skin, muscles, bone marrow

bulgur
cheese
eggs
fish
meat, especially beef, chicken, lamb, pork, veal; kidney, liver
milk
nuts
rice (brown)
rolled oats
yeast (brewer's, debittered)

Folic Acid
Beneficial to: appetite; red blood cells, skin, hair

chicken
kidney
legumes, especially black-eyed peas, lima beans
liver
orange juice
potatoes
turnips
vegetables (dark green and leafy), especially asparagus, beet greens, broccoli, chard, endive, kale, spinach
wheat bran, wheat germ
yogurt

Vitamin C (ascorbic acid)
Beneficial to: healing of wounds; bones, skin, teeth, tendons, connective tissue, red blood cells

Vitamins and Minerals

citrus fruits and juices, especially grapefruit,
  oranges
fruits, especially blueberries, cantaloupe,
  guava, honeydew, papaya, strawberries
lima beans
vegetables (green and green leafy), especially
  asparagus, broccoli, Brussels sprouts,
  cabbage, cauliflower, collards, green and
  red peppers, kale, kohlrabi, mustard
  greens, rutabaga, spinach, turnip greens
potatoes (cooked in jacket)
sweet potatoes (cooked in jacket)
tomatoes, tomato juice

Vitamin D
Beneficial to: absorption of calcium; teeth, bones
butter
egg yolks
fish (salt-water), especially herring, salmon,
  sardines, tuna
fish-liver oils (cod, halibut)
liver
milk (enriched)
Note: Direct sunlight on the skin acts to change cholesterol in the skin to vitamin D.

Vitamin E
Beneficial to: reproduction, healing of wounds; red blood cells; acts an an antioxidant
cereals (whole grain), especially rice, wheat,
  oats
cheese
eggs
fish and shellfish
margarine
meats, especially liver
milk
peanuts
rice

Vitamins and Minerals

    vegetable oils (wheat germ, cottonseed,
      safflower)
    vegetables, especially asparagus, broccoli,
      cabbage, spinach

Vitamin K
Beneficial to: blood clotting
    cabbage
    cauliflower
    kale
    spinach

MINERALS

Calcium
*Beneficial to: blood clotting; bones, teeth,
heart, nervous system*
    artichokes
    beans (dry, green, or waxed), especially lima
      beans, soybeans
    cereals (whole grain)
    cheeses, especially cheddar, cottage cheese,
      cheese foods and spreads
    cream
    custard
    eggs
    fish, especially salmon (canned with bones)
    fruits, especially blackberries, oranges,
      raspberries, rhubarb, tangerines
    ice cream
    milk, yogurt
    molasses
    pudding
    shellfish, especially clams, oysters, shrimp
    vegetables, especially beet greens, broccoli,
      cabbage, chard, collards, cress, dandelion
      greens, okra, kale, kohlrabi, mustard
      greens, parsnips, rutabaga, spinach,
      turnips, turnip greens, winter squash

Vitamins and Minerals

Copper
Beneficial to: metabolism, absorption of iron; red blood cells
- beans (dried)
- brains
- cocoa powder
- heart
- kidney
- liver (beef and pork)
- margarine (corn oil)
- molasses
- mushrooms
- nuts
- shellfish, especially oysters
- soybeans

Fluorine
Beneficial to: teeth, bones
- fish
- foods grown or cooked with fluoridated water
- most animal foods
- tea
- vitamins supplied with fluoride (for forming teeth)
- water supplied with fluoride

Iodine
Beneficial to: thyroid gland
- fish (salt-water)
- milk
- salt (iodized)
- seafood
- sea salt
- seaweed

Iron
Beneficial to: red blood cells, muscles
- beans (dried)
- cereals and breads (whole grain)
- egg yolks
- fruits (dried), especially apricots, prunes, raisins

meats (lean, red), especially heart, kidney,
   liver
molasses
peas (dried)
shellfish
vegetables (dark green and leafy)

Magnesium
*Beneficial to: metabolism; nervous system,
muscles*

bananas
beans (dried)
cereals and breads (whole grain)
eggs
milk
nuts, especially almonds, cashews, peanuts
peanut butter
seeds
soybeans
vegetables (dark green and leafy, raw)

Phosphorus
*Beneficial to: bones, teeth, kidneys, heart,
muscles*

beans (dried)
eggs
fish
food processed with phosphates
meat, especially liver, and poultry
milk and milk products
peas (dried)
soybeans
yeast (brewer's, debittered)

Potassium
*Beneficial to: heart, nervous system, muscles,
cells*

beans (dried)
bran
cocoa
coffee

Vitamins and Minerals

fish
fruits (fresh), especially avocado, bananas,
    cantaloupe, oranges
fruits (dried), especially raisins
grapefruit juice
meats, especially beef
milk
mushrooms
nuts
orange juice
peanut butter
peanuts
potassium salts and supplements
potatoes
tea
tomato juice
vegetables, especially beet greens, broccoli,
    Brussels sprouts, carrots, celery, chard,
    collards, lettuce, parsley, peas, spinach,
    squash, tomatoes

Zinc
*Beneficial to: metabolism of protein; muscles,
blood, hormones*

beans (dried)
cereals (whole grain)
cheese
cocoa
eggs
meat, especially liver
milk
nuts
poultry
seafood, including shellfish, especially oysters

Basic Weight Loss

General recommendations for a sensible weight-loss diet resemble the guidelines for a healthy, balanced diet. They involve eating a variety of foods but reducing the number of calories consumed. The easiest way to accomplish this is to choose lower-calorie foods, eat less fat, eat no more than three egg yolks a week, eliminate foods containing refined and processed sugars and flours, and reduce salt and alcohol. Eat more roughage or fiber, including whole grains and other complex carbohydrates such as fresh fruits and vegetables. Increasing fiber will increase the bulk of a diet and help to provide a feeling of fullness without adding concentrated calories. Eat beef and pork sparingly; choose instead poultry, fish, and veal, which contain less total fat and less saturated fat and cholesterol than pork or beef. Dairy products should be low fat or skimmed to reduce saturated fats, cholesterol, and calories.

Eat a variety of the proper foods in moderation: four or more servings per day from the whole grains (bread/cereal), beans, and nut groups; four or more servings per day from the fruits and vegetables group; two–four (child three–four, adult two) servings per day from the dairy products group (low-fat products only); and two servings per day from the meat group.

Exercising for a half hour to an hour a day will increase the number of calories burned. Cook foods plainly or season with spices, herbs, vinegar, or tart fruit juice instead of butter or fattening sauces; avoid fried foods. Budget calories by eating a little less at some meals to allow extra calories for parties and special occasions; eat raw fruits or vegetables for snacks. *But do not skip meals.* Following such

Basic Weight Loss

a program should help to form eating patterns that can be relied on to maintain desired weight. Consult the chart on pages 250–51 to determine your ideal weight.

Two restricted-calorie diets, with seven-day menu plans for each, appear on pages 27–34. Generally, the 1200-calorie diet should allow weight loss at a moderate to fast rate, while the 1800-calorie diet would be appropriate for slower loss and for maintenance after weight loss. But remember that each individual, depending on sex, body size, and activity level, has a different calorie requirement. Determining your own caloric level often involves some experimentation. Trial and error will help you to establish how much food you can eat and still lose or stabilize weight.

A weight loss of 1½ to 2 pounds a week is considered reasonable and safe. In general, adult males tend to lose excess weight faster than adult females. If you experience the so-called dieter's plateau, a stretch of time during which you lose no weight although you continue to follow your eating plan faithfully, try to remember that such a slowdown is usually only temporary. Adhere to your program of sensible, nutritionally sound dieting and you will reach your goal.

7-DAY MENU PLAN—1200 Calories *

SUNDAY

calories, 1200; protein, 54 gr.; fat, 65 gr.

Breakfast	**Lunch**
½ grapefruit	1 cup marinated
1 egg, scrambled in 1 tsp. oil	vegetables (marinade with 2 tsp. oil)
½ whole-wheat bagel	2 oz. cheese
1 tsp. margarine	1 whole-wheat roll
	1 pear

Dinner

3 oz. fresh pork roast
½ cup unsweetened applesauce
4–6 small new potatoes boiled in skin
1 tsp. margarine
½ cup three-bean salad (dressing with 2 tsp. oil)

MONDAY

calories, 1250; protein, 55 gr.; fat, 48 gr.

Breakfast	**Lunch**
4 oz. orange juice	1 cup vegetable soup
½ cup oatmeal	sandwich: 2 slices
1 cup skim-milk yogurt	whole-wheat bread,
1 tsp. honey	2 tbs. peanut butter
½ cup sliced strawberries	

Dinner

3 oz. roast chicken, without skin
½ cup bread stuffing
½ cup carrot and raisin salad
½ cup steamed broccoli
1 tsp. margarine

* All margarine is from corn oil; all oil is corn oil.
  Optional: plain coffee, tea, dietetic beverages

7-DAY MENU PLAN—1200 Calories

TUESDAY

calories, 1223; protein, 56 gr.; fat, 39 gr.

Breakfast	**Lunch**
½ cup orange sections	1 cup fruit salad
½ cup granola cereal	sandwich: 2 slices
8 oz. skim milk	whole-wheat bread,
	3 oz. chicken,
	4 tsp. mayonnaise

Dinner

1 cup black beans
1 cup yellow rice
hot sauce
tossed salad: lettuce, ½ cup raw vegetables,
    2 tsp. oil, vinegar, spices

WEDNESDAY

calories, 1270; protein, 64 gr.; fat, 65 gr.

Breakfast	**Lunch**
½ cup grapefruit juice	sandwich: 2 slices
1 soft-cooked egg	pumpernickel
1 slice whole-wheat toast	bread, 2 oz. turkey,
1 tsp. margarine	1 tbs. mayonnaise
	8 oz. skim milk

Dinner

veal scallopini: 3 oz. veal, 4 tbs. bread crumbs,
    2 tbs. oil, ½ cup mushrooms
½ cup steamed green beans
1 slice French bread

7-DAY MENU PLAN—1200 Calories

THURSDAY

calories, 1256; protein, 52 gr.; fat, 72 gr.

Breakfast	Lunch

Breakfast

4 oz. orange juice
1 bran muffin
1 tbs. peanut butter

Lunch

chef salad: lettuce, 1 cup raw vegetables, 1 oz. turkey, 1 oz. cheese, 2 tbs. oil, vinegar, spices
1 whole-wheat roll

Dinner

1½ cup beef stew with ½ cup noodles
½ cup tomato salad
1 tbs. oil
1 slice watermelon

FRIDAY

calories, 1200; protein, 55 gr.; fat, 62 gr.

Breakfast

½ cup bran cereal
1 banana
8 oz. skim milk

Lunch

cheese, tomato, and lettuce sandwich: pita bread, 2 oz. cheese, 1 tbs. mayonnaise

Dinner

3 oz. baked halibut with 1 tbs. margarine
1 cup zucchini salad
2 tbs. yogurt dressing
1 cup brown rice

7-DAY MENU PLAN—1200 Calories

SATURDAY

calories, 1226; protein, 40 gr.; fat, 60 gr.

Breakfast

½ cup orange and
  grapefruit sections
2 whole-wheat pancakes
  (6″ diam.)
1 tbs. syrup
4 oz. skim milk

Lunch

½ cup grape juice
tuna salad: 2 oz. tuna,
  2 tbs. mayonnaise
1 slice whole-wheat
  bread

Dinner

1 cup pasta
½ cup tomato sauce
1 meatball
green salad (dressing to include 1 tsp. oil)

7-DAY MENU PLAN—1800 Calories *

SUNDAY

calories, 1805; protein, 70 gr.; fat, 99 gr.

Breakfast	**Lunch**
½ grapefruit	2 cups marinated
1 egg, scrambled in	vegetables (mari-
1 tbs. oil	nade with 1 tbs. oil)
1 whole-wheat bagel	2 oz. cheese
2 tsp. margarine	1 whole-wheat roll
8 oz. skim milk	1 tsp. margarine
	1 pear

Dinner

3 oz. fresh pork roast
6 small new potatoes boiled in skin
1 tbs. margarine
½ cup three-bean salad (dressing with 2 tsp. oil)
½ cup ice cream

MONDAY

calories, 1774; protein, 76 gr.; fat, 66 gr.

Breakfast	**Lunch**
4 oz. orange juice	1 cup vegetable soup
½ cup oatmeal with	sandwich: 2 slices
1 tbs. honey	whole-wheat bread,
1 cup fruit yogurt	2 tbs. peanut butter
	8 oz. skim milk
	1 apple

Dinner

4 oz. roast chicken with 1 cup stuffing
½ cup carrot and raisin salad
steamed broccoli
1 tsp. margarine
½ cup tapioca pudding

---

* All margarine is from corn oil; all oil is corn oil.
  Optional: plain coffee, tea, dietetic beverages

7-DAY MENU PLAN—1800 Calories

TUESDAY

calories, 1787; protein, 63 gr.; fat, 67 gr.

Breakfast

1 cup orange sections
1 cup granola cereal
8 oz. skim milk

Lunch

1 cup fruit salad
sandwich: 2 slices
    whole-wheat bread,
    3 oz. chicken,
    2 tbs. mayonnaise
4 oatmeal cookies
    (2½″ diam.)

Dinner

1 cup black beans with 1 cup yellow rice
hot sauce
tossed salad: lettuce, ½ cup raw vegetables, 1 tbs. oil,
    vinegar, spices
1 slice black bread

WEDNESDAY

calories, 1797; protein, 79 gr.; fat, 90 gr.

Breakfast

½ cup grapefruit juice
1 soft-cooked egg
2 slices whole-wheat toast
1 tbs. margarine

Lunch

sandwich: 2 slices
    pumpernickel, 3
    oz. turkey, 1 tbs.
    mayonnaise
8 oz. skim milk
4 chocolate-chip
    cookies (2½″ diam.)

Dinner

veal scallopini: 3 oz. veal, 4 tbs. bread crumbs,
    2 tbs. oil, ½ cup mushrooms
½ cup steamed green beans
1 tbs. slivered almonds
2 slices French bread

7-DAY MENU PLAN—1800 Calories

THURSDAY

calories, 1787; protein, 68 gr.; fat, 99 gr.

Breakfast

4 oz. orange juice
2 bran muffins
2 tbs. peanut butter

Lunch

salad: lettuce, 1 cup raw
vegetables, 2 oz. tur-
key, 1 oz. cheese, 2
tbs. oil, vinegar, spices
2 whole-wheat rolls
2 tsp. margarine

Dinner

2 cups beef stew with 1 cup noodles
½ cup tomato salad
1 tbs. oil
1 slice watermelon

FRIDAY

calories, 1834; protein, 78 gr.; fat, 106 gr.

Breakfast

1 cup bran cereal
1 banana
8 oz. skim milk

Lunch

cheese, tomato, and
lettuce sandwich: pita
bread, 3 oz. cheese,
1 tbs. mayonnaise

Dinner

4 oz. baked halibut, with 2 tbs. margarine
1 cup zucchini salad
2 tbs. yogurt dressing
1 cup brown rice
½ cup baked custard

7-DAY MENU PLAN—1800 Calories

SATURDAY

calories, 1842; protein, 70 gr.; fat, 74 gr.

Breakfast

½ cup orange and
   grapefruit sections
4 whole-wheat pancakes
   (6" diam.)
2 tbs. syrup
4 oz. skim milk

Lunch

1 cup grape juice
tuna salad sandwich:
   2 slices whole-
   wheat bread, 3 oz.
   tuna, 2 tbs.
   mayonnaise

Dinner

2 cups pasta
¾ cup tomato sauce
2 meatballs
green salad (dressing with 1 tbs. oil)

Low-Sodium Diet

Sodium is a mineral that occurs naturally in foods. Forty percent of table salt is sodium. The National Research Council has determined that 1100–3000 milligrams of sodium daily is acceptable for healthy adults. The actual human requirement for sodium is only 250 milligrams per day, or one-tenth of a teaspoon. The average American consumes 2½ teaspoons every day—25 times the needed amount and more than twice the acceptable level!

A high sodium intake has been associated with a number of serious diseases, such as high blood pressure, and reducing sodium intake is considered prudent for everyone. However, limiting sodium is difficult because salt is added to most commercially processed and prepared foods, and it occurs naturally in others. An increased awareness of the dangers of too much sodium has begun to influence methods of food processing, and more and more foods are being offered in unsalted or low-salt forms. Always read the ingredients on labels and packages.

Foods Allowed

Dairy Products
    butter, margarine (unsalted)
    cheese (unsalted)
    milk (fresh)

Fats
    any unsalted (preferably low cholesterol)

Fruits—raw, with seeds, skins, and membrane when possible
    all fruits and fruit juices (no commercially
        prepared juices)

Grains and Grain Products
    breads, crackers, rolls, and other baked

goods (preferably whole grain) made
without salt, baking powder, baking soda,
or self-rising flour (salt-free baking powder
permitted)
cereals (any unsalted, preferably whole grain)
cornstarch
pasta and pasta-type foods (unsalted):
macaroni, noodles, spaghetti
rice (unsalted)
tapioca

Eggs

Meat—unsalted, fresh only, one serving daily
fish
heart
lean meat: beef, lamb, pork (fresh), veal;
poultry
liver
shellfish (clams, oysters, and shrimp only)

Sugars and Starches
chocolate (bitter or sweet, plain, unsalted)
cocoa powder
desserts (any prepared without salt),
including puddings or dairy desserts made
with milk
gelatin (unsalted)
honey
jam, jelly
maple syrup
marmalade (without sodium preservative)
sugar and plain sugar candy (unsalted)

**Vegetables—raw, with seeds, skins, and strings when
possible; canned or frozen, use sodium-free**
All vegetables are suitable, but choose only
one serving daily from among the
following:
artichokes
beet greens

Low-Sodium Diet

beets
carrots
celery (no dried celery products)
chard
collards
dandelion greens
kale
mustard greens
potato (unsalted only)
spinach
turnips
watercress

Miscellaneous
broth (unsalted)
cereal beverage
coffee
flavoring extracts
herbs
lemonade
meat sauce (unsalted)
mustard (one serving daily)
nuts (unsalted)
peanut butter (unsalted)
pepper
popcorn (unsalted only)
soft drinks (without sodium content)
soups (homemade)
spices (no seasoning salts, flavoring agents,
or mixed spices)
tea
vinegar
white sauce (unsalted)

Foods to Avoid

Breadstuffs
pretzels
salted crackers

Low-Sodium Diet

Dairy Products
- buttermilk
- canned milk
- chocolate or malted milk drinks, mixes, or syrups

Meats
- bacon
- cold cuts
- commercially prepared fish
- ham
- ham hocks
- hot dogs
- organ meats (except heart and liver)
- sausage

Miscellaneous
- baking soda
- barbecue sauce
- canned or packaged soups
- catsup
- cheese spread
- commercially prepared juices
- flavoring agents
- garlic salt
- meat tenderizers
- mixed spices
- olives
- onion salt
- pickles
- potato chips
- relish
- seasoning salts
- soy sauce

Vegetables
- commercially frozen lima beans, peas
- dried legumes
- hominy

Low-Carbohydrate Diet

Although nutritionists and physicians believe that the healthiest diet contains more complex carbohydrates and reduced amounts of fats, meats, and other protein foods, some people find that reducing carbohydrates for short periods of time can be an effective way of losing weight. It is important to remember that a low-carbohydrate diet excludes many foods and thus does not contain adequate amounts of a number of nutrients.

Two types of carbohydrates are starches and sugars. Starches are called complex carbohydrates, and sugars are called simple carbohydrates. Carbohydrates from foods in their natural state are called natural carbohydrates, while those that are processed from natural foods are called refined carbohydrates. All dairy products, fruits, grains and grain products, legumes, and vegetables contain carbohydrates, as do several food additives and flavorings. Complex carbohydrates in their natural state, close to their natural state, or with minimum processing are preferred because they take longer to metabolize, releasing glucose into the bloodstream slowly. Refined carbohydrates, such as white flour and white sugar, require little digestion, metabolize quickly, and release large amounts of glucose into the body all at once. They contain calories but few nutrients.

Develop the habit of reading the ingredients and nutritional information on the labels of packaged foods. If a refined or processed food has a sweetener—such as sucrose, dextrose, or just sugar—listed as the first, second, or third ingredient, then that food will have a high caloric level in relation to nutritional value.

Low-Carbohydrate Diet

Foods Allowed

Fats
no carbohydrates
  oils, lard, cooking fat (vegetable), imitation
    margarine, and animal fat—in reasonable
    amounts
low carbohydrates
  butter
  margarine

Dairy Products (all contain carbohydrates in varying amounts; low fat preferred)
  cheese
  milk (no nondairy substitutes)

Eggs

Fruits (all contain carbohydrates)
  all—fresh, raw, unprocessed, with seeds,
    skins, membrane; canned, water pack, no
    added sweeteners (no dried fruits or fruit
    juices)

Grain (whole grains only; all contain carbohydrates)
  all whole grains, whole-grain mixes, or whole-
    grain products, unrefined or unprocessed
    (no white flours, sugars, processed cereals,
    or processed foods)

Legumes, Nuts, Seeds (all contain carbohydrates)
  beans (dried)
    all
  nuts (dried)
    all kinds—with skins, dried, unprocessed,
      without added sugars and oils
  peas (dried)
    whole preferred
  seeds (dried)
    all—unhulled when possible, dried,
      unprocessed, without added sugars and
      oils

Low-Carbohydrate Diet

Meats

> *no carbohydrates*
> most meats, fish, and poultry (preferably
>   lean)
> *low carbohydrates*
> abalone
> bacon
> bologna, cold cuts, luncheon meats
> brains
> canned beef
> chipped beef
> cured hams
> fish roe
> frankfurters
> gefilte fish
> gizzard (chicken and turkey)
> herring
> organ meats (heart, kidney, liver, tongue, etc.)
> potted meats
> prepared meat dinners and soups
> shellfish (all types)
> sardines
> sausage (all types)
> squid

Sugars and Starches (all contain carbohydrates)

> carob products (no refined ingredients)
> desserts made with whole grains and other
>   high-fiber products (no refined ingredients)
> honey (unprocessed)
> molasses (unprocessed)
> raw sugar

**Vegetables (all contain varying amounts of
carbohydrates)**

> all—unprocessed, raw or barely cooked, with
>   seeds, skins, and strings when possible

Miscellaneous (some contain carbohydrates)

> baking powder (no aluminum)
> baking soda

Low-Carbohydrate Diet

bouillon, broth, or consommé
carbonated drinks and other soft drinks
   (artificially sweetened)
catsup
cereal beverage
club soda
coffee
gelatin (plain)
herbs
horseradish
mint
mustard
pectin
pepper
pickles (dill or sour)
rennet
salad dressings
salt (table and seasoned)
soups (none creamed)
spices
tea
thickeners: arrowroot, buttermilk, cornstarch,
   miller's bran, potato flour, tapioca, whole-
   grain flour, yogurt
vanilla extract, other extracts
vinegar
yeast (dry)

High-Protein Diet

Protein, necessary for growth and regeneration of the tissues as well as for resistance to disease, is not stored in the body and must be eaten several times daily. Not as much protein is required in the diet as was once thought, and some nutritionists believe that people frequently consume more protein than they need. The recommended daily allowance for protein is .36 grams per pound of body weight.

All animal protein is complete; that is, it contains the eight amino acids essential to our bodies. Vegetable protein is incomplete; that is, it lacks one or more of these essential amino acids. The protein supplied by soybeans is the closest to animal protein.

If the diet is based largely or totally on plant protein, as in the case of vegetarians, it is necessary to provide a nutritional balance, either by combining those plant proteins whose amino acids complement each other or by including alternative animal protein sources such as dairy products (see Complementary Proteins, below). Since most meat and dairy products have high fat content as well as protein, it is advisable, when on a weight-reducing diet, to choose the low-fat items like poultry, veal, seafood, and low-fat or skim dairy products and to combine vegetables and grains as protein sources.

In the following listing of foods allowed on a high-protein diet, complete and incomplete protein sources are identified. There is also a guide to protein foods that are complementary; combining any two or all of them as indicated will provide more complete protein or higher-quality protein.

High-Protein Diet

Complete Protein

Meat—moderate servings, lean preferred
fish (any)
meats (any)
organ meats
poultry
shellfish

Dairy Products—preferably low fat or skim
buttermilk
cheese
milk
yogurt

Eggs
no more than 3 a week

Incomplete Protein

Grain
bran and bran products (preferably
    unprocessed)
gluten products
rice, rice germ, and rice products (preferably
    brown rice or wild rice)
wheat germ
whole grains (barley, buckwheat, carob, corn,
    millet, oats, rice, rye, soy, wheat), whole-
    grain mixes, or whole-grain products in
    breads, cereals, crackers, muffins, rolls

Legumes, Nuts, Seeds
garbanzos (chickpeas)
kidney beans
lentils
lima beans
nuts, especially brazils, cashews, peanuts
    (preferably unprocessed)
peanut butter
peas (dried)
pinto beans (dried)

seeds (preferably unprocessed), including
  sesame seeds and sunflower seeds
soybeans

Vegetables—preferably raw, with seeds, skins, and strings when possible
  bean pods
  bean sprouts
  corn
  leafy vegetables
  potatoes and other root vegetables
  tofu (bean curd)

Complementary Proteins

broccoli, peas, and cauliflower with nuts
cheese with any or all foods; used in cooking
  and baking, in salads, as snacks
corn and cornmeal with legumes, dairy
  products, eggs; used in cooking and
  baking: cereals, casseroles, breads
dairy products such as milk, buttermilk,
  yogurt, and cheese with rice, wheat,
  cereals, corn, soy peanuts, sesame seeds,
  legumes, potatoes, gelatin; used in cooking
  and baking, in salads and salad dressing,
  as a beverage or snack
eggs (preferably only 3 a week) in cooking
  and baking: casseroles, omelets, desserts;
  in salads
fresh green vegetables with grains such as
  rice or millet
gelatin with dairy products; used in salads
  and desserts
grains, nuts, and seeds with legumes or dairy
  products
legumes with dairy products, rice, grains,
  corn, nuts and seeds; used in casseroles
  and salads, as snacks

High-Protein Diet

mushrooms with green peas, lima beans,
    Brussels sprouts, broccoli, cauliflower
nuts and seeds with dairy products, cereals,
    legumes, grains; used in cooking and
    baking, in salads, as snacks
peanuts with dairy products, soybeans, wheat,
    rice, breads, cereals; used in cooking and
    baking
potatoes with dairy products; used in
    casseroles, in salads, as snacks
rice (preferably brown) with fish, dairy
    products, legumes, soybeans, wheat; used
    in casseroles, salads, desserts
sesame seeds with dairy products, legumes,
    soybeans, walnuts, wheat breads, cereal;
    used in cooking and baking, in salads, as
    snacks
sesame seeds, Brazil nuts, and cashews with
    lima beans, green peas, cauliflower, and
    Brussels sprouts
soybeans with rice, wheat, corn, dairy
    products, sesame seeds, peanuts; used in
    casseroles and salads, as snacks
turkey (best of all meats and poultry) as a
    supplement to plant protein
whole grains and whole-grain mixes with
    seafood, legumes, dairy products, seeds,
    nuts; used in cooking and baking, as cereal
    and snacks

No-Protein Foods

fruits—all, preferably raw, with seeds, skins,
    and membrane when possible
sugars and starches

Low-Cholesterol Diet

We get cholesterol in two ways. Our bodies produce it in limited amounts, and we also ingest cholesterol, which is present in all foods of animal origin. Some cholesterol is necessary for good health. Too much cholesterol in the blood forms plaques on the walls of blood vessels, which can both reduce the size of the vessels and inhibit their proper functioning—contributing, in many cases, to atherosclerosis. High blood cholesterol may also be associated with heart disease.

When blood cholesterol levels are high, they can be reduced or stabilized by lowering the amount of cholesterol and saturated fats in the diet. This can be accomplished by limiting animal fats, hydrogenated vegetable fats, and coconut or palm oil. Do not eat more than three eggs a week, including those used as ingredients in other foods. Skim the fat off stews, soups, and gravies. Choose low-fat dairy products.

Foods Allowed

Dairy Products—low fat only; no nondairy substitutes
buttermilk
cheese
skim milk, yogurt

Eggs
egg white or cholesterol-free egg powder (no more than 3 egg yolks a week)

Fats and Oils—polyunsaturated and of vegetable origin only
corn oil, cottonseed oil
margarine (except completely hydrogenated); should have polyunsaturated fat listed first, as tub margarine with liquid safflower oil or liquid corn oil as the first ingredient, or stick margarine made with liquid corn oil

Low-Cholesterol Diet

    mayonnaise made only with foods permitted
    nuts (walnuts, pecans, almonds)
    safflower oil
    salad dressings made only with allowable
        foods
    sesame oil
    soybean oil
    sunflower oil
    vegetable shortening (except completely
        hydrogenated); in cooking or baking
        substitute ⅔ cup of polyunsaturated oil for
        each cup of solid shortening or butter

**Fruit—preferably raw, with skins, seeds, and
membrane when possible**
    all fruits and fruit juices

Grains and Grain Products
    breads, quick breads, and rolls
    cereals
    crackers
    flour (all)
    grain products prepared without butter,
        cream, hydrogenated fat, dried egg or egg
        yolks, whole milk, butter, cheese, or any
        foods not permitted (no commercial mixes
        containing foods not permitted)
    grains (all)
    pastry made with vegetable shortening

**Meats—baked, broiled, roasted, stewed, or fried in
allowable fats; lean only, without visible fat or skins**
    beef (not smoked)
    fish (not smoked)
    fowl (not smoked)
    lamb
    meat extracts
    turkey (not smoked)
    veal

Sugars and Starches
    cakes without cream, butter, chocolate,
        coconut, or egg yolks

candy without cream, butter, chocolate,
    coconut, or egg yolks
cookies without cream, butter, chocolate,
    coconut, or egg yolks
desserts or sweets without butter, chocolate,
    coconut, cream, dried eggs or egg yolk,
    hydrogenated fats, whole milk, nuts, ice
    cream or ice milk, or any other item not
    allowed, including additives such as BHT
gelatin desserts
honey
ices
jams
jellies
molasses
pectin
preserves
puddings made with allowable foods
sherbet
sugars
sweet rolls made with allowable foods
syrups

Vegetables—preferably raw, with seeds, skins, and strings when possible
    all vegetables, especially eggplant, onions,
        potatoes, soybeans
    potato substitutes prepared with allowable
        foods
    vegetable soup (without fat)

Miscellaneous
    broth (clear)
    carbonated beverages
    cereal beverages
    coffee
    condiments
    flavoring extracts
    garlic
    herbs
    pickles

popcorn prepared with allowable fats
salt
soups (fat free) made with allowable foods
spices
tea
vinegar
white sauce made with allowable foods

Bland Diet

A bland diet is often recommended medically for some types of digestive problems, such as ulcers and colitis. It is designed to eliminate foods that irritate the digestive tract or increase acid production in the stomach. Reactions to foods will vary from person to person. If a certain food causes distress, it should be removed from the diet. Raw fruits, vegetables, or nuts and seeds do not necessarily have to be avoided on a bland diet. Many Mexican and Italian dishes contain ingredients that may cause digestive discomfort; approach them— and all highly spiced foods—with discretion.

Foods to Avoid

Beverages

alcoholic drinks (beer, liquor, wine)
coffee
cocoa
soft drinks containing cola
tea

Spices

chili powder
nutmeg
pepper

High-Fiber Diet

Diets high in fiber are beneficial for a number of reasons. Fiber, also called roughage or bulk, helps reduce the amount of sugar and fat in the bloodstream and facilitates the proper functioning of the digestive system, speeding the elimination of waste products.

High-fiber diets also encourage weight loss because the foods that are high in roughage, usually complex carbohydrates, have fewer calories than no-fiber foods like meats, take longer to chew, and provide a feeling of fullness that is satisfying.

The crude fiber content on product labels may not indicate true fiber content, because true fiber content has been analyzed for only a few foods. Dairy products and meats do not contain fiber.

It is important to drink plenty of liquids while on a high-fiber diet. Occasionally, an increase in fiber in the diet may result in excessive flatulence. This condition can often be avoided by increasing the amount of fiber gradually.

Foods Allowed

Fruit
    all fresh berries and fruits—raw, with seeds, skins, and membrane when possible
    dried fruits: apricots, currants, dates, figs, peaches, pears, prunes, raisins, etc.
    fruit juices

Grain
    barley
    breads (whole grain)
    buckwheat groats (kasha)
    bulgur (cracked wheat)

High-Fiber Diet

cereals (whole grain), especially barley, 100% bran, 40% or 100% bran flakes, buckwheat, hot cereals, granola cereals, dry, rolled, or puffed oats, rye flakes, wheat (flakes, shredded)

chips (taco, tortilla) and shells (enchiladas, tacos, tortillas, tostadas) made from whole-ground corn

crackers, muffins, pancakes, pasta, pastry, rolls, waffles made with whole-grain flour

flour (whole grain), such as buckwheat, carob, cornmeal, 100% rye, soy, wheat—unprocessed or barely milled

flour products, anything with whole grains

matzo meal (whole-wheat)

miller's bran or wheat bran

popcorn

rice (brown or wild)

rice bran

rice cakes (puffed, formed)

wheat (100% stone ground)

Legumes, Nuts, Seeds

beans (dried)
  bayo
  black
  brown
  calico
  garbanzos (chickpeas)
  lentils
  lima
  pinto
  red
  soybeans
  white
  yellow

nuts (dried)
  all—unprocessed, without added sugars or oils
  peanut butter (without additives)

peas (dried)
    any (whole peas preferred)
seeds (dried)
    all—unprocessed, without added sugars or
    oils

Sugars and Starches
carob products
desserts made with whole grains and other
    high-fiber products

Vegetables
all—unprocessed, raw or barely cooked and
    including seeds, skins, and strings when
    possible

Vegetarian Diet

A vegetarian is someone who eats no meat, fish, or poultry. There are three basic types of vegetarians. Those whose diet includes dairy products and eggs are called lacto-ovo-vegetarians. Vegetarians who omit eggs but include milk products are known as lacto-vegetarians. Vegetarians who do not eat any animal products are called vegans.

As with any diet, it is important to consume enough quality protein to ensure growth and maintenance of the body. Eggs and dairy products supply a high-quality protein with all the essential amino acids. Therefore, lacto-ovo-vegetarians and lactovegetarians normally are provided with adequate proteins and are not at risk of developing protein deficiency. Vegans, however, must take care to eat vegetable proteins in certain combinations (see page 45) in order to provide their bodies with the essential amino acids.

Vitamin B_{12} is found only in animal products. Within five to ten years on a strict vegetarian diet that includes no animal products, a person may develop a vitamin B_{12} deficiency. A varied diet with dairy products and eggs will ensure an adequate supply of all vitamins and minerals. The following list of foods can be adapted for use by the three types of vegetarians.

Foods Allowed

Vegetables
    all—raw, with seeds, skins, and strings when possible, as much as you want, as many as 6 meals a day

Fruit
    all—raw, with seeds, skins, and membranes when possible

Nuts
all—with skins

Dairy Products
all

Eggs

Grains and Grain Products
all (whole)

Legumes

Diabetic Diet

Persons with diabetes, a disease that affects the body's ability to metabolize carbohydrates, must have careful medical supervision. The occurrence of diabetes usually requires some change in the patient's eating patterns. Determining the appropriate regimen for each individual is a very complicated procedure, but most physicians prescribe a modified carbohydrate diet that avoids concentrated sweets to aid in controlling the blood-sugar level. Diets for diabetics are based on the individual patient's need for a specific caloric intake that includes protein, fat, and carbohydrates, determined by height, ideal weight, activity, sex, and age. Diabetes in some overweight adults may be controlled by diet and weight reduction alone. For others, insulin may have to be taken to metabolize sugar.

The recommended foods are usually distributed among three daily meals and one to three snacks. Meals are usually planned for specific times, and it is essential to eat at approximately the same time every day. It is very important not to omit meals. Often a midmorning snack or a snack before exercising is advisable, and a snack before bed is frequently needed by those who are taking long-acting insulin. If a person who has diabetes vomits or rejects food, a physician should be contacted immediately.

Initially, foods should be measured before cooking (until judging portion sizes becomes second nature) and then baked, broiled, boiled, or roasted. If foods are fried, the fat allowance must be used for that purpose.

The individual diet will usually have exchange lists of recommended foods with specified amounts that can be eaten each day from each list. Select only from these lists. Foods within the same list are interchangeable because they contain approximately the same amounts of carbohydrates, proteins, and fats. The food categories include fat exchanges, meat exchanges, fruit exchanges, vegetable exchanges, bread exchanges, milk exchanges, and a group of miscellaneous foods. Anything not allowed on the prescribed diet should be avoided.

A booklet for meal planning, *Exchange Lists,* may be obtained by writing to the American Diabetes Association, 600 Fifth Avenue, New York, New York 10020.

Low-Residue Diet

Physicians sometimes recommend a low-residue or low-fiber diet for individuals with intestinal problems. Lowering fiber in a diet lowers the amount of bulk that must pass through the intestinal tract. Decreased bulk may help to prevent aggravation of any inflammation that is present. Foods low in vegetable fiber are allowed in this diet.

Foods Allowed

Beverages
  bouillon
  broth
  carbonated drinks
  coffee
  tea

Dairy Products
  cheeses
  cream sauce
  custards and puddings
  ice cream
  milk
  sherbets

Fats
  any except nuts and olives

Fruits—canned, cooked, fresh, or frozen without seeds, skins, or membranes
  avocado (ripe)
  banana (ripe)
  canned or cooked apples, apricots, cherries,
    peaches, pears
  juices without pulp

Grain and Grain Products—refined only
  breads (wheat, graham, rye)
  cakes and cookies (plain)
  cereals (ready to eat or cooked; no bran)

Low-Residue Diet

crackers (wheat, graham, rye)
flours
hominy grits
macaroni
noodles
quick breads and rolls
spaghetti

Eggs

Meats—tender only
bacon
fish
gravy
poultry

Sugars and Starches
candy (no coconut or nuts)
desserts and sweets (without nuts, coconut, fruits)
gelatin
jelly (no jam or marmalade)
sugar
syrups

Vegetables—in limited amounts, cooked without seeds, skins, or strings
asparagus
beets
carrots
cauliflower
chard
lettuce
mushrooms
potato or potato substitutes
pumpkin
spinach
squash
tomato (ripe)
other mild-flavored vegetables

Miscellaneous
  chocolate
  cocoa
  condiments (if tolerated)
  herbs
  peanut butter (smooth)
  salt
  soup (creamed, strained, with allowable
    vegetables)
  spices (no chili powder, cloves, garlic,
    pepper, pickles, seed spices)

Low-Purine Diet

The occurrence of gout—a metabolic disorder marked by painful inflammation of the joints, usually treated with a combination of drug therapy and diet—is associated with substances called purines. The swelling and pain of gout are caused by the accumulation of uric acid in the system. Most uric acid is formed in the body, and gout occurs either when too much of the acid is produced or when not enough is eliminated. One of the factors in uric-acid build-up is the body's inability to metabolize purines properly. Purines are found in certain protein foods, and physicians may prescribe that foods very high in purine be excluded from the gout sufferer's diet. Increased intake of fluids is helpful in eliminating uric acid, with a minimum of two quarts of fluid a day recommended.

Obesity has been associated with gout, and gradual weight loss is also recommended.

Foods Allowed

Dairy
any—preferably low fat including milk drinks

Fats
any (no bacon)

Fruit
any—preferably raw, with seeds, skins, and
membrane when possible

Grain
any—preferably whole grains and whole-
grain products

Meat and Fish
all fish and shellfish (except anchovies,
herring, mackerel, sardines, scallops)

all meats (except bacon, heart, kidney, liver,
   sweetbreads, broth and bouillon, meat
   extracts, commercially prepared soups and
   gravies; nothing fried)
meat substitutes (any dairy products,
   preferably low fat, including cottage
   cheese; eggs; peanut butter)
poultry (except goose, wild game)

Miscellaneous
   chocolate
   cocoa
   condiments
   herbs
   pickles
   salt
   spices
   vinegar
   white sauce

Sugars and Starches
   any

Vegetables
   any—preferably raw with seeds, skins, and
      strings when possible (no fried potatoes or
      potato chips)
   asparagus, spinach, peas (used sparingly)
   dried legumes and peas (used sparingly)

Liquid Diet

Some conditions require that solid foods be restricted for short periods of time. In such cases physicians may prescribe some type of liquid regimen: either clear liquids only or a full liquid diet including foods that liquefy at body temperature.

Some doctors prescribe for their patients a powdered food to mix with liquid. Sometimes people on weight-loss diets replace one or more solid meals with a liquid-formula diet. Each portion is generally 225 calories and is sold in cans or packages in supermarkets and pharmacies. Such a liquid diet is advisable for only a short period. Another form of liquid diet, the liquid protein diet, is not considered safe.

Clear Liquid Diet

Beverages
  bouillon (clear only)
  broth (clear only)
  cereal beverage (plain)
  clear carbonated drinks (such as ginger ale,
    lemon-flavored soda)
  coffee (plain)
  tea (plain)

Fruit
  fruit punch
  juices (apple, grape, cranberry)

Sugars and Starches
  fruit ice
  gelatin
  sugar
  sugar candy (plain)

Full Liquid Diet

Beverages
bouillon, broth
carbonated drinks
cereal beverage
coffee
milk and milk drinks
tea

Dairy Products
dry milk
half and half
milk and milk drinks

Fats
butter
margarine

Fruits
juices

Vegetables
tomato juice
vegetable juice

Grains
cereals (cooked)

Eggs
custard
dried egg powder
eggnog

Sugar and Starches (no coconut, nuts, whole fruit)
custard
gelatin
ice cream (vanilla or chocolate)
pudding
sherbet

Miscellaneous
cream soups (strained)
protein drinks (usually added to milk)

High-Potassium Diet

Potassium is a mineral that occurs naturally in foods. It has been estimated that most adults require 2500 milligrams of potassium daily, although no minimum allowance has been offically established. Some people may require extra potassium when they are taking certain medications under a physician's care.

The following is a list of foods high in potassium and the amount of it that they supply. These potassium-rich foods can be included in the diet when medical treatment calls for an increased amount of this nutrient.

Food	Potassium
½ cup raw chickpeas	787 mg
1 baked potato	782 mg
½ acorn squash	749 mg
½ cantaloupe	682 mg
1 cup spinach	583 mg
1 cup tomato juice	552 mg
1 cup tomatoes	523 mg
1 medium stalk broccoli	481 mg
1 cup orange juice	476 mg
1 banana	440 mg
1 cup grapefruit juice	400 mg
2 oz. peanuts	380 mg
1 cup milk	351 mg
½ cup red kidney beans	309 mg
1 orange	263 mg

Composition of Foods

The table that follows presents more than a thousand commonly eaten foods—in the forms that consumers find when shopping or dining out. The table gives the typical serving size for each food and then shows the amounts of the vital elements: calories, protein, fat, carbohydrate (including fiber), and sodium.

The foods are listed alphabetically, from abalone to zwieback. When there are several varieties of a general type of food, such as baby foods, beverages, or plate dinners, they are listed under the general heading.

Many commercially prepared combinations of foods are included. In this way you can see their entire composition immediately, and you will not have to guess or compute the composition of each element. For example, under plate dinners you can find the composition of a typical frozen dinner: meat loaf with tomato sauce, mashed potatoes, and peas.

For abbreviations used in the table and throughout the book see the list on page 255.

Composition of Foods*

Food	Amount	Calories
A		
Abalone		
uncooked	3.5 oz.	98
canned	3.5 oz.	80
Almonds, dried, unsalted	1 oz.	171
Apple, fresh	1 med.	85
Apple brown betty	approx. ½ c.	151
Apple butter	3.5 oz.	186
Apple juice		
canned or bottled	1 c.	117
frozen concentrate, unsweetened, diluted per directions	6 oz.	90
Applesauce		
sweetened	½ c.	117
unsweetened	½ c.	50
Apricot nectar	1 c.	144

dash (—) in a column indicates no reliable data even
though component may be present in a measurable
amount.

Protein (gr.)	Fat (gr.)	Carbohydrate (gr.)		Sodium** (mg)
		Total	Fiber	
18.7	.5	3.4	0	—
16.0	.3	2.3	0	—
5.3	15.5	5.6	.7	1
.5	1.0	20.5	1.5	2
1.6	3.5	29.7	.5	153
.4	.8	46.8	1.1	2
.3	trace	30.6	.3	3
0	0	22.0	—	—
.27	.1	30.6	.6	trace
.26	.3	13.3	.7	3
.8	.3	36.9	.5	1

*Some foods are labeled as follows: "low" (below 100 mg); "moderate" (100–250 mg); "high" (251–500 mg); "very high" (above 500 mg).

Food	Amount	Calories
Apricots fresh	3.5 oz.	51
canned, heavy syrup	1 c.	221
dried, uncooked	1 c.	393
Artichokes raw	1 lg. head	9–47 (varies fresh to stored)
cooked	3.5 oz.	8–44 (varies fresh to stored)
Asparagus spears, fresh, cooked	4 spears	12
frozen cuts and tips, cooked	1 c.	40
canned	1 c.	44
Avocado California	1	489
Florida	1	585

B

Food	Amount	Calories
Baby Foods—Cereals and cereal products, precooked, dry Barley	1 oz.	99
Farina, instant	1 oz.	16

Protein (gr.)	Fat (gr.)	Carbohydrate (gr.)		Sodium (mg)
		Total	Fiber	
1.0	.2	12.8	.6	1
1.5	.3	56.6	1	3
7.6	.7	4.8	4.5	39
2.9	.2	10.6	2.4	43
2.8	.2	9.9	2.4	30
1.3	.1	2.2	.4	1
5.8	.4	6.4	1.5	2
4.6	.8	7.1	1.2	581
6.3	46.6	17.1	4.3	11
5.9	50.2	40.2	6.9	18
3.8	.3	21.0	.3	129
.5	trace	3.3	trace	54

Food	Amount	Calories
Baby Foods—Cereals (cont.) High-protein	1 oz.	102
Mixed	1 oz.	105
Oatmeal	1 oz.	107
Rice	1 oz.	106
Teething biscuit	1 oz.	108
Baby Foods—Desserts, dinners, meats, poultry, eggs, commercially prepared in jars, bottles, or cans *Desserts* Custard pudding (all flavors)	3.5 oz.	100
Fruit pudding	3.5 oz.	96
Dinners (cereal, vegetable, meat mixtures, 2–4% protein) Beef noodle dinner	3.5 oz.	48
Cereal, egg yolk, and bacon	3.5 oz.	82
Chicken noodle dinner	3.5 oz.	49
Macaroni, tomatoes, meat, and cereal	3.5 oz.	67
Split peas, vegetables, and ham or bacon	3.5 oz.	80

Protein (gr.)	Fat (gr.)	Carbohydrate (gr.)		Sodium (mg)
		Total	Fiber	
10.1	1.1	13.7	.6	187
4.3	.8	20.2	.3	134
4.7	1.6	18.9	.4	125
1.9	.5	22.9	.1	151
3.2	.7	22.3	.2	120
2.3	1.8	18.6	.2	150
1.2	.9	21.6	.3	128
2.8	1.1	6.8	.3	269
2.9	4.9	6.6	.1	301
2.1	1.3	7.2	.1	297
2.6	2.0	9.6	.3	381
4.0	2.1	11.2	.2	295

Food	Amount	Calories
Baby Foods (cont.) **Meats, poultry, and eggs** Beef, junior	3.5 oz.	118
Beef, strained	3.5 oz.	99
Beef heart	3.5 oz.	93
Beef with vegetables	3.5 oz.	87
Chicken	3.5 oz.	127
Chicken with vegetables	3.5 oz.	100
Egg yolks, strained	3.5 oz.	210
Egg yolks with ham or bacon	3.5 oz.	208
Lamb, junior	3.5 oz.	121
Lamb, strained	3.5 oz.	107
Liver, strained	3.5 oz.	97
Liver and bacon, strained	3.5 oz.	123
Pork, junior	3.5 oz.	134

Protein (gr.)	Fat (gr.)	Carbohydrate (gr.)		Sodium (mg)
		Total	Fiber	
19.3	3.9	0	0	283
14.7	4.0	0	0	228
13.5	3.8	.4	0	208
7.4	3.7	6.0	.2	304
13.7	7.6	0	0	263
7.4	4.6	7.2	.2	265
10.0	18.4	.2	0	273
10.0	18.1	.3	0	313
17.5	5.1	0	0	294
14.6	4.9	0	0	241
14.1	3.4	1.5	0	253
13.7	6.6	1.3	0	302
18.6	6.0	0	0	237

Food	Amount	Calories
Baby Foods—Meats (cont.) Pork, strained	3.5 oz.	118
Turkey with vegetables	3.5 oz.	86
Veal, strained	3.5 oz.	91
Baby Foods—Fruits and fruit products, with or without thickening Applesauce	3.5 oz.	72
Applesauce and apricots	3.5 oz.	86
Bananas, strained, with tapioca or cornstarch, added ascorbic acid	3.5 oz.	84
Bananas and pineapple, with tapioca or cornstarch	3.5 oz.	80
Fruit dessert with tapioca (apricot, pineapple, and/or orange)	3.5 oz.	84
Peaches	3.5 oz.	81
Pears	3.5 oz.	66
Pears and pineapple	3.5 oz.	69
Plums with tapioca, strained	3.5 oz.	94
Prunes with tapioca	3.5 oz.	86

Protein (gr.)	Fat (gr.)	Carbohydrate (gr.)		Sodium (mg)
		Total	Fiber	
15.4	5.8	0	0	223
6.7	3.2	7.6	.5	348
15.5	2.7	0	0	226
.2	.2	18.6	.5	6
.3	.1	22.6	.5	—
.4	.2	21.6	.1	29
.4	.1	20.7	.1	59
.3	.3	21.5	.2	53
.6	.2	20.7	.5	—
.3	.1	17.1	1.0	4
.4	.2	17.6	.9	—
.4	.2	24.3	.3	38
.3	.2	22.4	.3	33

Food	Amount	Calories
Baby Foods—Vegetables		
Beans, green	3.5 oz.	22
Beets, strained	3.5 oz.	37
Carrots	3.5 oz.	29
Mixed vegetables (including vegetable soup)	3.5 oz.	37
Peas, strained	3.5 oz.	54
Spinach, creamed	3.5 oz.	43
Squash	3.5 oz.	25
Sweet potatoes	3.5 oz.	67
Tomato soup, strained	3.5 oz.	54
Bacon, Canadian broiled or fried, drained	1 slice (approx. 1/2 oz.)	58
Bacon, cured	20 slices per lb.	
broiled or fried, drained	2 slices	93
canned	1 oz.	196

Protein (gr.)	Fat (gr.)	Carbohydrate (gr.)		Sodium (mg)
		Total	Fiber	
1.4	.1	5.1	.8	213
1.4	.1	8.3	.6	212
.7	.1	6.8	.6	169
1.6	.3	8.5	.5	272
4.2	.2	9.3	.8	194
2.3	.7	7.5	.4	272
.7	.1	6.2	.8	292
1.0	.2	15.5	.5	187
1.9	.1	13.5	.2	294
5.7	3.7	.1	0	537
4.6	7.9	.5	0	155
2.4	20.4	.3	0	moderate to high

Food	Amount	Calories
Bagel Commercial, made with egg	1 (3" diam.)	165
Home recipe, made with water, all-purpose flour	1	180
Bamboo shoots, raw	1 c.	40
Bananas, fresh	1 med.	102
Barbecue sauce	1 tbs.	14
Barley, pearled light, uncooked	½ c.	352
pot or Scotch	½ c.	351
Bass, black sea baked, stuffed	3.5 oz.	259
Bass, smallmouth and largemouth uncooked	3.5 oz.	104
Bass, striped uncooked	3.5 oz.	105
oven-fried	3.5 oz.	196
Beans, common, mature seeds, dry White cooked	1 c.	303

Protein (gr.)	Fat (gr.)	Carbohydrate (gr.)		Sodium (mg)
		Total	Fiber	
6.0	2.0	28.0	—	245
5.0	0	38.0	—	550
4.0	.4	8.0	1.1	—
1.3	.3	26.6	.6	1
.2	1.1	1.3	.1	128
8.3	1.0	79.5	.5	3
9.7	1.1	77.9	.9	—
16.2	15.8	11.4	—	—
18.9	2.6	0	0	—
18.9	2.7	0	0	—
21.5	8.5	6.7	—	—
20.0	1.5	54.5	3.9	18

Food	Amount	Calories
Beans, white (cont.)		
canned (with pork and sweet sauce)	1 c.	385
canned (with pork and tomato sauce)	1 c.	313
Red		
cooked	1 c.	303
canned	1 c.	231
Pinto, calico, and red Mexican, raw	approx. ½ c.	349
Others including black, brown, and bayo, raw	approx. ½ c.	339
Beans, lima, immature seeds		
boiled, drained	1 c.	190
canned, drained solids	1 c.	165
Baby limas, frozen, cooked (thin-seeded)	1 c.	214
Fordhooks, frozen, cooked (thick-seeded)	1 c.	170
Beans, lima, mature seeds, dry		
cooked	1 c.	260
Beans, mung, sprouted seeds		
uncooked	1 c.	37
cooked	1 c.	35

Protein (gr.)	Fat (gr.)	Carbohydrate (gr.)		Sodium (mg)
		Total	Fiber	
15.9	12.0	54.2	4.4	976
15.6	6.7	48.8	3.6	1189
20.0	1.3	54.9	3.9	8
14.7	1.0	42.2	2.3	8
22.9	1.2	63.7	4.3	10
22.3	1.5	61.2	4.4	25
13.0	.9	34.0	3.1	2
9.2	.5	31.4	3.1	405
13.4	.4	40.4	3.4	234
10.3	.2	327	2.8	173
15.4	1.1	48.2	3.2	4
4.0	.2	7.0	.7	5
4.0	.3	6.6	.9	5

Food	Amount	Calories
Beans, snap		
Green		
cooked	1 c.	30
canned	1 c.	43
frozen, cut, cooked	1 c.	34
frozen, French-cut	1 c.	34
Yellow or wax		
cooked	1 c.	28
canned	1 c.	46
frozen, cooked, cut	1 c.	37
Beans and frankfurters, canned	1 c.	370
Beef, chipped		
uncooked	3.5 oz.	203
cooked, creamed	3.5 oz.	154
Beef, chuck cuts		
Arm, choice grade, braised or potroasted (85% lean, 15% fat)	3.5 oz.	289
Rib, 5th, choice grade, braised (69% lean, 31% fat)	3.5 oz.	427

Protein (gr.)	Fat (gr.)	Carbohydrate (gr.)		Sodium (mg)
		Total	Fiber	
2.0	.3	6.8	1.3	5
2.4	.3	10.1	1.4	568
2.2	.1	7.8	1.4	1
2.1	.1	7.8	1.4	3
1.8	.3	5.8	1.3	4
2.4	.5	10.1	1.4	568
2.3	.1	8.4	1.5	1
19.5	18.3	32.4	2.6	1386
34.3	6.3	0	0	4300
8.2	10.3	7.1	trace	716
27.1	19.2	0	0	60 (av.)
22.4	36.7	0	0	60 (av.)

Food	Amount	Calories
Beef, corned, boneless cooked	3.5 oz.	372
Beef, corned-beef hash canned	3.5 oz.	181
Beef, flank steak, choice grade braised (100% lean)	3.5 oz.	196
Beef, hamburger (ground beef) lean, cooked	3.5 oz.	219
regular, cooked	3.5 oz.	286
Beef, hind shank, choice grade simmered (66% lean, 34% fat)	3.5 oz.	361
Beef, loin end or sirloin Double-bone sirloin steak, choice grade, broiled (66% lean, 34% fat)	3.5 oz.	408
Hipbone sirloin steak, choice grade, broiled (55% lean, 45% fat)	3.5 oz.	487
Wedge and round-bone sirloin steak, broiled (66% lean, 34% fat)	3.5 oz.	387
Beef, loin or short loin Club steak, choice grade, broiled (58% lean, 42% fat)	3.5 oz.	454
Porterhouse steak, choice grade, broiled (57% lean, 43% fat)	3.5 oz.	465
T-bone steak, choice grade, broiled (56% lean, 44% fat)	3.5 oz.	473

Protein (gr.)	Fat (gr.)	Carbohydrate (gr.)		Sodium (mg)
		Total	Fiber	
22.9	30.4	0	0	1740
8.8	11.3	10.7	.5	540
30.5	7.3	0	0	60 (av.)
27.4	11.3	0	0	60 (av.)
24.2	20.3	0	0	60 (av.)
25.1	28.1	0	0	60 (av.)
22.2	34.7	0	0	60 (av.)
19.1	44.9	0	0	60 (av.)
23.0	32.0	0	0	60 (av.)
20.6	40.6	0	0	60 (av.)
19.7	42.2	0	0	60 (av.)
19.5	43.2	0	0	60 (av.)

Food	Amount	Calories
Beef, rib		
11th–12th, choice grade, roasted (55% lean, 45% fat)	3.5 oz.	481
6th or blade, choice grade, braised (70% lean, 30% fat)	3.5 oz.	437
Beef, round (entire), choice grade broiled (81% lean, 19% fat)	3.5 oz.	261
Beef, rump, choice grade roasted (75% lean, 25% fat)	3.5 oz.	347
Beef, short plate, choice grade simmered (58% lean, 42% fat)	3.5 oz.	474
Beef, stir-fried home recipe, with vegetable oil, soy sauce	1 c.	255
Beef and vegetable stew home recipe	1 c.	211
canned	1 c.	181
Beef pot pie	1 whole before baking	562
Beef stroganoff home recipe, with sour cream	4 oz.	735
Beef teriyaki home recipe, with soy sauce	4 oz.	429
Beer. *See* Beverages.		
Beet greens, boiled, drained	1 c.	26

Protein (gr.)	Fat (gr.)	Carbohydrate (gr.)		Sodium (mg)
		Total	Fiber	
18.3	44.7	0	0	60 (av.)
22.1	38.0	0	0	60 (av.)
28.6	15.4	0	0	60 (av.)
23.6	27.3	0	0	60 (av.)
20.6	42.8	0	0	60 (av.)
22.0	13.0	12.0	---	840
15.2	11.0	14.7	.9	88
13.3	7.1	16.2	.7	939
23.1	33.1	43.0	.9	649
27.0	55.0	31.0	---	768
21.0	35.0	7.0	---	1840
2.5	.3	4.8	1.6	111

Food	Amount	Calories
Beets		
boiled, drained	1 c.	32
canned, solids and liquid	1 c.	84
Beverages—Alcoholic and nonalcoholic carbonated		
Alcoholic		
Beer	8 fl. oz.	102
light (low-calorie) types	12 oz.	varies 96–134
Gin, rum, vodka, whiskey		
80-proof	1 fl. oz.	65
86-proof	1 fl. oz.	70
90-proof	1 fl. oz.	75
94-proof	1 fl. oz.	78
100-proof	1 fl. oz.	83
Wines		
dessert (alcohol 18.8% by volume, 15.3% by weight)	3.5 oz.	137
table (alcohol 12.2% by volume, 9.9% by weight)	3.5 oz.	85
Nonalcoholic, carbonated		
Club soda	8 fl. oz.	0.
Colas	8 fl. oz.	97

Protein (gr.)	Fat (gr.)	Carbohydrate (gr.)		Sodium (mg)
		Total	Fiber	
1.1	.1	7.3	.8	43
2.3	.3	19.6	1.2	585
.8	0	9.2	—	17
—	—	—	—	—
—	—	trace	—	trace
—	—	trace	—	trace
—	—	trace	—	trace
—	—	trace	—	trace
—	—	trace	—	trace
.1	0	7.7	—	4
.1	0	4.2	—	5
0	0	0	0	low
0	0	24.8	0	—

Food	Amount	Calories
Beverages, nonalcoholic (cont.) Cream sodas	8 fl. oz.	106
Diet sodas (with artificial sweetener), average type	8 fl. oz.	less than 1 per oz.
Fruit-flavored sodas and Tom Collins mixes	8 fl. oz.	115
Ginger ale	8 fl. oz.	76
Quinine water (sweetened)	8 fl. oz.	76
Root beer	8 fl. oz.	102
Seltzer	8 oz.	—
Sparkling water	8 oz.	—
Biscuits, baking powder home recipe	1 (approx. 2″ diam.)	104
made from biscuit mix, with milk	1 (approx. 2″ diam.)	92
Blackberries, boysenberries, dewberries, youngberries, fresh	1 c.	84
Black-eyed peas. *See* **Cowpeas and black-eyed peas.**		
Blueberries, fresh	1 c.	87

Protein (gr.)	Fat (gr.)	Carbohydrate (gr.)		Sodium (mg)
		Total	Fiber	
0	0	27.0	0	—
0	0	—	0	low
0	0	30.0	0	low
0	0	19.7	0	low
0	0	19.7	0	—
0	0	26.0	0	low
—	—	—	0	less than 10
—	—	—	0	5
2.1	4.8	13.0	.1	177
2.0	2.6	14.8	.1	275
1.7	1.3	18.7	5.9	2
1.0	.7	21.6	2.1	1

Composition of Foods

Food	Amount	Calories
Bluefish baked or broiled	3.5 oz.	159
Boston brown bread	approx. 1¾ oz.	102
Bouillon cube	1 cube	5
Bran cereal, all natural, quick-cooking	1 oz.	110
Bran flakes 40% bran, added thiamine	1 c.	106
With raisins, added thiamine	1 c.	144
Brazil nuts	1 oz.	187
Bread (average loaf) Cracked-wheat	1 slice	66
French or Vienna	1 slice	73
Italian	1 slice	69
Raisin	1 slice	66
Rye American	1 slice	61
pumpernickel	1 slice	62

Composition of Foods

Protein (gr.)	Fat (gr.)	Carbohydrate (gr.)		Sodium (mg)
		Total	Fiber	
26.2	5.2	0	0	104
2.7	.6	22.0	.3	121
.8	.1	.2	—	960
5.0	4.0	19.0	—	—
3.6	.6	28.3	1.3	325
4.2	.7	39.9	1.5	403
4.1	19.1	3.1	.9	trace
2.2	.6	13.1	.1	133
2.3	.8	13.9	.1	146
2.3	.2	14.2	.1	147
1.7	.7	13.5	.2	92
2.3	.3	13.1	1.0	140
2.3	.3	13.3	.3	143

Food	Amount	Calories
Bread (cont.) Sourdough, home recipe	1 slice	105
White, enriched	18 slices per av. loaf	
1–4% nonfat dry milk	1 slice	68
5–6% nonfat dry milk	1 slice	69
Whole-wheat	18 slices per av. loaf	
2% nonfat dry milk	1 slice	61
Bread crumbs dry, grated	1 c.	392
Bread pudding with raisins	½ c.	251
Bread stuffing Home recipe, made with butter, bread, chicken broth, salt	1 c.	194
Made from mix, prepared with water, egg, butter	approx. ½ c.	208
Brioche home recipe, made with all- purpose flour	1	138
Broccoli frozen, chopped, cooked	1 c.	48

Protein (gr.)	Fat (gr.)	Carbohydrate (gr.)		Sodium (mg)
		Total	Fiber	
3.0	2.0	19.0	—	70
2.2	.8	12.7	.1	127
2.3	1.0	12.6	.1	124
2.6	.8	12.0	.4	133
12.6	4.6	73.4	.3	736
7.5	8.2	38.1	.1	270
4.0	13.0	17.0	—	544
4.4	12.8	19.7	.2	501
4.0	5.0	19.0	—	104
5.4	.6	8.5	2.0	28

Food	Amount	Calories
Broccoli (cont.) whole stalks, med. size, cooked	1 stalk	47
Brussels sprouts fresh, boiled	1 c.	56
Butter	1 tbs.	100
Buttermilk 99% fat free, low salt	1 c.	90
Low fat (1.5% milk fat), no salt	1 c.	120
C		
Cabbage cooked, shredded	1 c.	29
raw, shredded	1 c.	14
Cake *Home recipe* Angel food	1 piece	144
Boston cream pie	1 piece	210
Chocolate with chocolate icing	1 piece	264
Fruit, with enriched flour	1 slice (1" x 1½" x ½")	56
Gingerbread, with enriched flour	1 piece	181

Protein (gr.)	Fat (gr.)	Carbohydrate (gr.)		Sodium (mg)
		Total	Fiber	
5.7	.6	8.2	2.7	18
6.6	.6	10.0	2.5	16
.1	11.3	.1	0	138
8.0	2.0	11.0	0	—
9.0	4.0	12.0	0	125
1.6	.8	6.3	1.2	20
.8	.1	3.0	.6	10
3.8	.1	32.2	0	151
3.5	6.5	34.7	0	129
3.2	11.7	39.9	.2	168
.85	2.3	8.2	.1	28
2.2	6.1	29.7	.1	135

Food	Amount	Calories
Cake, home recipe (cont.) Pound	1 slice	143
Sponge	1 piece	198
White with uncooked white icing	1 piece	268
Yellow with chocolate icing	1 piece	276
Frozen, packaged Devil's food with chocolate icing	1 piece	271
Made from mix Angel food	1 piece	138
Chocolate malt with uncooked white icing	1 piece	247
Coffeecake	1 piece	234
Cupcake	1 (2½" diam.)	88
with chocolate icing	1	130
Devil's food with chocolate icing	1 piece	235
Gingerbread	1 piece	175
Honey spice with caramel icing	1 piece	251

Protein (gr.)	Fat (gr.)	Carbohydrate (gr.)		Sodium (mg)
		Total	Fiber	
1.7	8.9	14.2	trace	33
5.1	3.8	36.0	0	111
2.4	9.2	44.9	0	167
3.2	9.8	45.7	.2	157
3.1	12.6	39.7	.2	300
3.0	.1	31.7	trace	78
2.4	6.2	47.6	.1	227
4.6	7.0	38.0	.1	312
1.2	3.0	14.0	.1	114
1.6	4.6	21.5	.1	122
3.1	8.5	40.5	.2	182
2.0	4.3	32.4	trace	193
2.9	7.7	43.5	.1	175

Food	Amount	Calories
Cake, made from mix (cont.) Marble with boiled white icing	1 piece	236
White with chocolate icing	1 piece	251
Yellow with chocolate icing	1 piece	234
Cake icings *Home recipe* Caramel	1 tbs.	62
Chocolate	1 tbs.	64
Coconut	1 tbs.	38
White uncooked	1 tbs.	75
boiled	1 tbs.	19
Made from mix Chocolate fudge	1 tbs.	65
Creamy fudge	1 tbs.	52
Candy Butterscotch	1 oz.	113
Caramels, plain or chocolate	1 oz.	114
with nuts	1 oz.	122

Protein (gr.)	Fat (gr.)	Carbohydrate (gr.)		Sodium (mg)
		Total	Fiber	
3.1	6.2	44.3	.1	185
2.8	7.7	44.9	.2	162
2.8	7.8	40.0	.1	158
.2	1.1	13.1	0	14
.5	2.4	.2	.1	10
.2	.8	7.9	.1	13
.1	1.3	16.3	0	10
.1	0	4.8	0	9
.4	2.5	11.5	.1	27
.4	1.0	11.5	.1	36
trace	1.0	27.1	0	19
1.1	2.9	21.9	.1	65
1.3	4.7	20.1	.1	58

Food	Amount	Calories
Candy (cont.) Caramels, chocolate-flavored roll	1 oz.	113
Chocolate bittersweet	1 oz.	136
semisweet	1 oz.	145
sweet	1 oz.	151
milk, plain	1 oz.	149
milk, with almonds	1 oz.	152
milk, with peanuts	1 oz.	155
Chocolate bar milk, plain	1 (av. 1.5 oz.)	220
milk, with crisped rice	1 (av. 2 oz.)	320
chewy type, with milk chocolate, corn syrup, cocoa, salt	1 small (av. .7 oz.)	90
Chocolate-covered: almonds	1 oz.	163
chocolate fudge	1 oz.	123
chocolate fudge with nuts	1 oz.	129

Protein (gr.)	Fat (gr.)	Carbohydrate (gr.)		Sodium (mg)
		Total	Fiber	
.6	2.3	23.6	.1	56
2.3	11.3	13.4	.5	1
1.2	10.2	16.3	.3	1
1.3	10.0	17.0	.1	9
2.2	9.2	16.3	.1	27
2.7	10.2	14.7	.2	23
4.0	10.9	12.7	.3	19
3.0	13.0	23.0	—	40
4.0	18.0	38.0	—	low
.5	3.0	15.0	—	low
3.5	12.5	11.3	.4	17
1.1	4.6	20.9	.1	65
1.4	5.9	19.2	.1	59

Food	Amount	Calories
Candy, chocolate-covered (cont.) coconut center	1 oz.	125
fudge, caramel, and peanuts	1 oz.	128
honeycombed hard candy, with peanut butter	1 oz.	132
mint	1 oz.	117
nougat and caramel	1 oz.	119
peanuts	1 oz.	160
raisins	1 oz.	121
vanilla creams	1 oz.	124
Chocolate-flavored roll, chewy type	1 oz.	115
Fudge chocolate	1 oz.	114
chocolate with nuts	1 oz.	122
vanilla	1 oz.	114
vanilla with nuts	1 oz.	121

Protein (gr.)	Fat (gr.)	Carbohydrate (gr.)		Sodium (mg)
		Total	Fiber	
.8	5.0	20.6	.2	56
2.5	5.9	17.5	.15	48
1.9	5.6	20.1	.1	47
.5	3.0	23.1	trace	53
1.1	4.0	20.8	.1	49
4.7	11.8	20.1	.2	18
1.5	4.9	20.1	.2	18
1.1	4.9	20.1	trace	52
—	—	—	—	6
.8	3.5	21.4	.1	54
1.1	5.0	19.7	.1	49
.9	3.2	21.4	0	59
1.2	4.7	19.7	.1	53

Food	Amount	Calories
Candy (cont.) Gumdrops	1 oz.	99
Hard candies	1 oz.	110
Jellybeans	1 oz.	105
Marshmallows	5 lg.	97
Mints, uncoated	1 oz.	104
Peanut bars	1 oz.	147
Peanut brittle	1 oz.	120
Sugar-coated almonds	1 oz.	130
Carrots cooked	1 c.	45
raw	1 med.	21
Cashew nuts roasted in oil, unsalted	1 oz.	160
dry roasted, salted	1 oz.	160
Cauliflower cooked	1 c.	27

Protein (gr.)	Fat (gr.)	Carbohydrate (gr.)		Sodium (mg)
		Total	Fiber	
trace	.2	25.0	0	10
0	.3	27.8	0	9
trace	.1	26.6	trace	3
.6	trace	24.3	0	12
trace	.6	25.6	trace	61
5.0	9.2	13.5	.3	3
1.6	3.0	23.1	.1	9
2.2	5.3	20.1	.3	6
1.3	.3	10.4	1.5	48
.5	.1	4.9	.5	24
4.9	13.1	8.4	.4	4
—	—	—	—	220
2.8	.3	4.9	1.2	11

Food	Amount	Calories
Caviar, pressed (sturgeon)	1 oz.	90
Celery		
cooked, diced	1 c.	28
raw (8" x 1½" at root)	1 med. stalk	7
raw, diced	1 c.	17
Cereal. *See* Bran cereal; Bran flakes; Corn products; Granola; Oat products; Rice products; Wheat products.		
Chard, Swiss		
raw	1 c.	42
cooked	1 c.	36
Charlotte russe with ladyfingers, whipped cream	3.5 oz.	286
Cheese		
Natural		
Blue or Roquefort type	1 oz.	105
Brick	1 oz.	106
Brie (domestic)	1 oz.	90
Camembert (domestic)	1 oz.	85

Protein (gr.)	Fat (gr.)	Carbohydrate (gr.)		Sodium (mg)
		Total	Fiber	
9.8	4.8	1.4	—	high to very high
1.6	.2	6.3	1.2	177
.4	trace	1.6	.2	51
.9	.1	3.9	.6	126
4.0	.5	7.6	1.3	245
3.6	.4	6.6	1.4	172
5.9	14.6	33.5	trace	43
6.1	8.7	.6	0	very high
6.3	8.7	.5	0	moderate
5.0	8.0	1.0	0	—
5.0	7.1	.5	0	high

Food	Amount	Calories
Cheese (cont.) Cheddar (domestic)	1 oz.	114
Cottage creamed or regular (4% milk fat)	½ c.	120
uncreamed (dry, less than ½% milk fat)	½ c.	100
low fat (1% milk fat)	½ c.	83
Cream	1 oz.	107
Feta (domestic)	1 oz.	100
Limburger	1 oz.	99
Mozzarella with whole milk	1 oz.	90
with part-skim milk	1 oz.	80
Parmesan	1 oz.	112
Provolone	1 oz.	100
Ricotta with whole milk	½ c.	215
with part-skim milk	½ c.	170

Protein (gr.)	Fat (gr.)	Carbohydrate (gr.)		Sodium (mg)
		Total	Fiber	
7.1	9.2	.6	0	700
15.6	4.8	3.2	0	260
19.6	.4	3.2	0	332
14.0	1.0	3.0	0	high
2.3	10.8	.6	0	71
10.0	8.0	1.0	0	—
6.1	8.0	.6	0	high
6.0	7.0	1.0	0	—
8.0	5.0	1.0	0	—
10.3	7.4	.8	0	210
7.0	8.0	1.0	0	—
14.0	16.0	3.5	0	low
14.0	9.5	6.5	0	low

Food	Amount	Calories
Cheese (cont.)		
Swiss		
domestic	1 oz.	106
imported	1 oz.	100
Pasteurized process		
American	1 oz.	106
Cheese food (American)	1 oz.	92
Cheese spread (American)	1 oz.	82
Pimiento (American)	1 oz.	106
Swiss	1 oz.	101
Cheese fondue	3.5 oz.	265
Cheese soufflé	3.5 oz.	218
Cherries, maraschino	1 oz.	33
Cherries, sour		
red, fresh	1 c.	58
canned, water pack	1 c.	106
Cherries, sweet		
fresh	10 cherries	48

Protein (gr.)	Fat (gr.)	Carbohydrate (gr.)		Sodium (mg)
		Total	Fiber	
7.9	8.0	.5	0	203
8.0	9.0	0	0	—
6.6	8.6	.5	0	326
5.7	6.9	2.0	0	high to very high
4.6	6.1	2.3	0	464
6.6	8.6	.5	trace	very high
7.5	7.7	.5	0	333
14.8	18.3	10.0	trace	542
9.9	17.1	6.2	trace	364
.1	1.0	8.4	.1	—
1.2	.3	14.3	.2	2
2.0	.5	26.3	.3	5
.9	.2	11.9	.3	1

Food	Amount	Calories
Cherries, sweet (cont.) canned, water pack	1 c.	116
Chestnuts fresh	1 oz.	55
Chicken All types light meat without skin, roasted	3.5 oz.	166
dark meat without skin, roasted	3.5 oz.	176
Broiler, flesh only, broiled	3.5 oz.	136
Fryer flesh and skin, fried	3.5 oz.	250
flesh only, fried	3.5 oz.	209
Roaster flesh and skin, roasted	3.5 oz.	248
flesh only, roasted	3.5 oz.	183
Chicken, canned meat only	3.5 oz.	198
Chicken, fried frozen	4.5 oz.	350
Chicken, stewed home recipe	1 c.	165
Chicken, stir-fried home recipe, with vegetable oil and soy sauce	1 c.	200

Protein (gr.)	Fat (gr.)	Carbohydrate (gr.)		Sodium (mg)
		Total	Fiber	
2.2	.5	28.8	.7	2
.8	.4	12.0	.3	2
31.6	3.4	0	0	64
28.0	6.3	0	0	86
23.8	3.8	0	0	66
30.6	11.9	2.8	—	low to moderate
31.2	7.8	1.2	—	78
27.1	14.7	0	0	—
29.5	6.3	0	0	376
21.7	11.7	0	0	—
23.0	19.0	20.0	0	865
25.0	5.0	2.0	0	200
20.0	10.0	9.0	0	700

Food	Amount	Calories
Chicken à la king home recipe	1 c.	471
Chicken and noodles home recipe	1 c.	370
Chicken cacciatore home recipe, with tomatoes, peppers, mushrooms	1 serv.	320
Chicken fricassee home recipe	3.5 oz.	161
Chicken Kiev home recipe, fried in oil	4–5 oz.	330
Chicken potpie home recipe	⅓ of 9″ pie	549
frozen	1 pie (approx. 8 oz. before baking)	501
Chickpeas (garbanzos)	3.5 oz.	360
Chicory Greens, raw	1 c.	11
Head, bleached (Witloof)	2 oz.	9
Chili con carne canned, with beans	1 c.	335
canned, without beans	1 c.	514

Protein (gr.)	Fat (gr.)	Carbohydrate (gr.)		Sodium (mg)
		Total	Fiber	
27.6	34.6	12.4	trace	765
22.5	18.6	25.9	trace	604
25.0	10.0	25.0	0	1030
15.3	9.3	3.2	trace	154
30.0	20.0	10.0	0	200
23.4	31.6	42.8	.9	598
15.3	26.3	50.7	.9	939
20.5	4.8	61.0	5.0	26
1.0	.2	2.2	.5	—
.6	.1	1.8	—	4
18.9	15.3	30.8	1.5	1338
26.5	38.1	14.9	.5	very high

Food	Amount	Calories
Chili con carne (cont.)		
home recipe, with rice and beans	1 c.	400
Chili sauce. *See* **Tomato chili sauce.**		
Chipped beef. *See* **Beef, chipped.**		
Chocolate, bitter or baking	1 oz.	144
Chocolate syrup		
thin type	1 tbs.	47
fudge type	1 tbs.	63
Chop suey		
canned, with meat	1 c.	156
home recipe, with meat	1 c.	302
Chow mein, chicken		
canned	1 c.	96
home recipe	1 c.	257
Clams		
Raw		
soft-shelled (steamer)	3.5 oz.	82
hard-shelled (quahog)	3.5 oz.	80
Canned	3.5 oz.	98

Protein (gr.)	Fat (gr.)	Carbohydrate (gr.)		Sodium (mg)
		Total	Fiber	
30.0	10.0	50.0	—	860
3.1	15.1	8.26	.7	1
.4	.4	12.0	.1	10
1.0	2.5	10.3	.1	17
11.1	8.0	10.6	2.0	1389
26.2	17.1	12.9	1.2	1061
6.5	.3	17.9	.8	731
31.2	10.1	10.1	.8	723
14.0	1.9	1.3	—	36
11.1	.9	5.9	—	205
15.8	2.5	1.9	—	—

Food	Amount	Calories
Cocoa and chocolate-flavored beverage powders Cocoa powder with nonfat dry milk	1 oz.	103
without milk	1 oz.	99
Packaged mix	1 oz.	112
Coconut meat fresh	1 oz.	99
dried, sweetened, shredded	1 oz.	157
Cod broiled	3.5 oz.	170
canned	3.5 oz.	85
dried, salted	3.5 oz.	130
Coffee Fresh-brewed	1 c.	2
Instant, prepared with water regular	1 c	—
decaffeinated	1 c.	—
with flavorings, sweetened	1 c. (2 rounded tsp.)	60 av.
Cold cuts. *See* Sausage, cold cuts, and luncheon meats.		

Protein (gr.)	Fat (gr.)	Carbohydrate (gr.)		Sodium (mg)
		Total	Fiber	
5.3	.8	20.0	.1	150
1.1	.6	25.5	.3	77
2.7	3.0	21.1	.2	109
1.0	10.1	2.7	1.1	7
1.0	11.2	15.2	1.2	low
28.5	5.3	0	0	110
19.2	.3	0	0	—
29.0	.7	0	0	very high
trace	trace	trace	trace	2
—	—	—	0	1
—	—	—	0	1
0–1	2–3	7–10	0	20–95

Food	Amount	Calories
Coleslaw made with salad dressing	3.5 oz.	99
Collards boiled	1 c.	56
Cookies *Home recipe* Brownies with nuts	1	98
Chocolate chip	1	52
Packaged Animal crackers	4	48
Chocolate	1	44
Chocolate chip	1	47
low-sodium type	1	25
Coconut, low-sodium type	1	25
Coconut bars	1	47
Fig bars	1	50
Gingersnaps	4	119
Graham crackers plain	4	109

Protein (gr.)	Fat (gr.)	Carbohydrate (gr.)		Sodium (mg)
		Total	Fiber	
1.2	7.9	7.1	.7	124
5.2	1.1	9.4	1.5	48
1.3	6.3	10.3	.1	51
.5	3.0	6.0	trace	35
.7	1.0	8.9	trace	34
.7	1.6	7.1	trace	14
.5	2.1	7.0	trace	40
trace	1.0	3.0	—	5
trace	1.0	3.0	—	less than 5
.6	2.3	6.0	.1	14
.5	.8	10.6	.2	35
1.6	2.5	22.6	trace	161
2.3	2.7	20.7	.3	190

Food	Amount	Calories
Cookies, graham crackers (cont.) chocolate-coated	1 lg.	71
Ladyfingers	4	159
Macaroons	2	182
Marshmallow	1	75
Molasses	1	100
Oatmeal with raisins	2	119
Peanut	1	74
Raisin	1	53
Sandwich-type, chocolate or vanilla, with creamy filling	1	50
Shortbread	6	213
Sugar, soft, thick	1	105
Sugar wafers, layered, with filling	1	43
Vanilla wafers	5	94

Protein (gr.)	Fat (gr.)	Carbohydrate (gr.)		Sodium (mg)
		Total	Fiber	
.8	3.5	10.1	.1	60
3.5	3.5	28.6	trace	31
2.0	8.9	25.3	.8	13
.7	2.4	13.2	.1	38
1.5	2.5	18.0	trace	92
1.6	4.0	19.3	.1	43
1.6	3.0	10.5	.1	27
.6	.7	11.3	.1	7
.5	2.3	6.9	trace	48
3.1	9.9	27.9	.1	26
1.4	4.0	16.1	trace	75
.4	1.7	6.5	trace	17
1.1	3.3	15.1	trace	51

Food	Amount	Calories
Cookies, vanilla wafers (cont.) low-sodium type	1	25
Coq au vin home recipe, with butter, bacon, onions, mushrooms, burgundy	1 serv.	270
Corn, sweet fresh, cooked on the cob	1 med. ear	71
fresh kernels, cooked	1 c.	214
canned, cream style	1 c.	212
canned (wet pack), whole kernel	1 c.	170
frozen, cooked on the cob	1 med. ear (corn only)	119
frozen kernels	1 c.	156
Corn bread home recipe, Southern style, with butter or bacon drippings	1 piece	79
made from mix, with egg and milk	1 piece	83
Corned beef. *See* Beef, corned.		
Corn fritters	3.5 oz.	377

Protein (gr.)	Fat (gr.)	Carbohydrate (gr.)		Sodium (mg)
		Total	Fiber	
trace	1.0	3.0	—	less than 5
25.0	10.0	10.0	—	210
2.6	.8	16.3	.5	trace
8.3	2.6	48.5	1.8	trace
5.4	1.5	51.6	1.3	609
4.9	1.5	40.5	1.5	609
4.4	1.3	27.4	.9	1
5.8	1.7	35.9	1.2	2
2.5	2.1	12.2	.1	208
2.2	3.0	11.8	trace	266
7.8	21.5	39.7	.5	477

Food	Amount	Calories
Corn grits cooked	1 c.	126
Corn products—Packaged, used mainly as ready-to-eat breakfast cereals Corn flakes plain	1 c.	97
sugar-coated	1 c.	156
Puffed corn	1 c.	81
presweetened	1 c.	115
presweetened, cocoa or fruit flavor	1 c.	119
Cornstarch	1 tbs.	27
Cowpeas and black-eyed peas immature seeds, cooked	1 c.	174
young pods, with seeds, cooked	3.5 oz.	34
mature seeds, dry, cooked	1 c.	191
Crab Steamed blue, Dungeness, rock, king	3.5 oz.	93
Canned	3.5 oz.	101

Protein (gr.)	Fat (gr.)	Carbohydrate (gr.)		Sodium (mg)
		Total	Fiber	
2.9	.3	27.1	.3	506
2.0	.1	21.4	.1	253
1.8	.1	36.8	.2	312
1.6	.9	16.4	.1	215
1.2	1.0	2.7	.1	91
1.8	.75	26.4	1.5	182–257
trace	trace	6.5	trace	trace
13.0	1.3	29.2	2.9	2
2.6	.3	7.0	1.7	3
12.9	.8	34.8	2.6	20
17.3	1.9	.5	—	high
17.4	2.5	1.1	—	1000

Food	Amount	Calories
Crab (cont.) Deviled made with bread, butter, eggs, catsup	3.5 oz.	188
Crab apple	1	68
Crackers Animal. *See* Cookies.		
Butter	4	60
Cheese	10 bits	70
Graham. *See* Cookies.		
Rye wafers	2	45
Saltines	4	49
Sandwich-type, cheese, with peanut-butter filling	6	210
Soda	3	89
Whole-wheat	4	36
Cranberries fresh	1 c.	55
Cranberry juice cocktail	1 c.	164

Protein (gr.)	Fat (gr.)	Carbohydrate (gr.)		Sodium (mg)
		Total	Fiber	
11.4	9.4	13.3	—	867
.4	.3	17.8	.6	1
.9	2.3	8.8	trace	144
1.6	3.1	8.8	trace	151
1.7	.2	10.0	.3	116
1.0	1.3	8.0	trace	123
6.5	10.2	24.0	.2	425
1.9	2.7	14.3	trace	223
.7	1.2	6.0	.2	48
.5	.8	12.9	1.7	2
.3	.3	41.5	trace	3

Food	Amount	Calories
Cranberry-orange relish uncooked	1 oz.	51
Cranberry sauce canned, strained, sweetened	1 c.	408
Cream Half and half	1 tbs.	20
Heavy, whipping unwhipped	1 tbs.	53
whipped	2 tbs.	53
Light, coffee or table	1 tbs.	32
Light, whipping unwhipped	1 tbs.	45
whipped	2 tbs.	45
Cream puffs with custard filling	1	233
Cream substitute powdered	1 tsp.	1
Croissant Home recipe, whole-wheat	1	170
Packaged	1 (2 oz.)	200
Cucumber	1 med. (7½" x 2")	43

Protein (gr.)	Fat (gr.)	Carbohydrate (gr.)		Sodium (mg)
		Total	Fiber	
.1	.1	13.0	—	trace
.3	.6	105	.6	3
.5	1.8	.7	0	7
.3	5.7	.5	0	5
.3	5.7	.5	0	5
.5	3.1	.7	0	7
.4	4.7	.5	0	5
.4	4.7	.5	0	5
6.5	13.9	20.5	trace	83
.2	.5	1.2	0	12
3.0	11.0	15.0	—	245
4.0	13.0	19.0	—	310
2.6	.3	9.7	1.7	17

Food	Amount	Calories
Currants Black, European	3.5 oz.	54
Red and white	3.5 oz.	50
Custard, baked home recipe	approx. ½ c.	115

D/E

Food	Amount	Calories
Dandelion greens cooked	1 c.	60
Dates	5	110
Doughnuts cake type	1	126
yeast-leavened	1	208
Duck domestic, flesh only, raw	3.5 oz.	165
wild, flesh only, raw	3.5 oz.	138
Eclairs with custard filling and chocolate icing	1	219
Eel, American smoked	3.5 oz.	330
Eggplant boiled	1 c.	38

Protein (gr.)	Fat (gr.)	Carbohydrate (gr.)		Sodium (mg)
		Total	Fiber	
1.7	.1	13.1	2.4	3
1.4	.2	12.1	3.4	2
5.4	5.5	11.1	0	79
3.6	1.1	11.6	2.3	80
.9	.2	29.4	.9	trace
1.5	6.0	16.6	trace	162
3.2	13.4	19.0	.1	118
21.4	8.2	0	0	74
21.3	5.2	0	0	—
5.7	12.4	21.2	trace	75
18.6	27.8	0	0	—
2.0	.4	8.2	1.8	2

Food	Amount	Calories
Eggplant (cont.) stuffed with onion and pepper, home recipe	approx. ⅓ c.	160
Eggplant parmigiana home recipe, with Italian-style tomato sauce, bread crumbs, cheese	approx. 5 oz.	370
Eggs, chicken, large	1	82
fried	1	109
hard-boiled or soft-boiled	1	82
omelet	2	173
poached	1	82
scrambled	2	173
white only	1	17
yolk only	1	60
Endive (curly) and escarole, raw	1 c.	11

F

Farina cooked	1 c.	106

Protein (gr.)	Fat (gr.)	Carbohydrate (gr.)		Sodium (mg)
		Total	Fiber	
3.0	12.0	10.0	—	235
15.0	25.0	20.0	—	670
6.5	5.8	.5	0	61
6.9	8.6	trace	0	170
6.5	5.8	.5	0	61
11.2	12.9	2.4	0	257
6.4	5.8	.4	0	136
11.2	12.9	2.4	0	257
3.6	trace	.3	0	48
2.7	5.2	.1	0	9
1.0	.1	2.3	.5	8
3.2	.3	21.9	trace	469

Food	Amount	Calories
Fettuccine home recipe, with spinach noodles, bacon, Parmesan cheese	1 c.	465
Fettuccine noodles home recipe, made with spinach	¾ c.	100
Figs canned (light syrup), solids and liquids	½ c.	79
dried	1 lg.	58
fresh	1 lg.	48
Filberts (hazelnuts) unsalted	1 oz.	181
Finnan haddie	3.5 oz.	103
Fish. *See* individual names.		
Fish cakes frozen, fried	3.5 oz.	270
Fish sticks cooked	5 sticks	201
Flatfish, uncooked	3.5 oz.	79
Flounder, baked	3.5 oz.	202

Protein (gr.)	Fat (gr.)	Carbohydrate (gr.)		Sodium (mg)
		Total	Fiber	
24.0	23.0	40.0	—	980
4.0	2.0	16.0	—	210
.6	.3	20.3	.8	2
.9	.3	14.6	1.2	7
.7	.2	12.3	.7	1
3.6	178.3	4.8	.9	1
23.2	.4	0	0	2
9.2	17.9	17.2	—	very high
19.0	10.2	7.4	—	very high
16.7	.8	0	0	78
30.0	8.2	0	0	237

Food	Amount	Calories
Frankfurters Beef	approx. 1.5 oz.	140
Chicken	2 oz.	140
See also Sausage, cold cuts, and luncheon meats.		
Frankfurters and beans. *See* Beans and frankfurters.		
French toast home recipe, with white bread, syrup	2 slices	700
Frozen dinners. *See* Plate dinners.		
Fruit cocktail, heavy syrup	½ c.	98
Fruit salad, canned water pack	½ c.	43
heavy-syrup pack	½ c.	96

G

Food	Amount	Calories
Garlic salt	1 tsp.	—
Gelatin desserts made with water plain	1 c.	142
with fruit	1 c.	170

Protein (gr.)	Fat (gr.)	Carbohydrate (gr.)		Sodium (mg)
		Total	Fiber	
5.0	13.0	1.0	0	460
7.0	11.0	2.0	0	—
10.0	13.0	140.0	—	550
.5	.1	25.4	.5	6
.5	.1	11.2	.6	1
.4	.1	24.8	.5	1
—	—	—	—	1850
3.6	0	34.0	0	123
3.3	.3	41.6	.5	86

Food	Amount	Calories
Goose flesh and skin, roasted	3.5 oz.	441
flesh only, roasted	3.5 oz.	233
Gooseberries fresh	1 c.	63
canned, heavy syrup	3.5 oz.	90
Granola Home recipe, with oats, coconut, nuts, dried fruit, brown sugar, honey, vegetable oil	1 c.	650
Packaged, with almonds and seeds	1 oz.	120
Granola bars home recipe	1 (3″ x 1″)	70
Grapefruit canned, syrup pack	½ c.	90
fresh, white, pink, or red	½ med.	99
Grapefruit juice Fresh white, pink, or red	1 c.	97
Canned unsweetened	1 c.	102
sweetened	1 c.	134

Protein (gr.)	Fat (gr.)	Carbohydrate (gr.)		Sodium (mg)
		Total	Fiber	
22.9	38.1	0	0	high
33.9	9.8	0	0	124
1.3	.3	15.6	3.0	2
.5	.1	23.0	1.2	1
10.0	30.0	90.0	—	135
5.0	4.0	17.0	—	—
1.0	4.0	7.0	—	70
.8	.1	22.8	.3	1
1.2	.3	25.8	.5	2
1.2	.3	23.0	trace	2
1.2	.3	24.4	trace	2
1.2	.3	32.3	trace	3

Food	Amount	Calories
Grapefruit juice (cont.) Frozen concentrate, unsweetened, diluted per directions	1 c.	100
Grapefruit juice and orange juice blended unsweetened	1 c.	107
sweetened	1 c.	125
Grape juice canned or bottled	1 c.	168
frozen concentrate, sweetened, diluted per directions	1 c.	135
Grapes American type (Concord, Delaware, Niagara, Catawba, scuppernong), fresh	1 c.	106
European type, fresh	1 c.	108
Canned, syrup pack	1 c.	186
Gravy Cream, for fried chicken, home recipe, with milk	1/3 c.	152
Pan, home recipe, with all-purpose flour	1/4 c.	62
Grits. *See* Corn grits.		
Guavas	1	53

Protein (gr.)	Fat (gr.)	Carbohydrate (gr.)		Sodium (mg)
		Total	Fiber	
1	trace	24.0	—	—
1.5	.5	25.2	.2	2
1.2	.2	30.5	.2	2
1.0	trace	42.0	—	—
1.0	trace	33.0	—	—
2.0	1.5	24.2	.9	5
1.0	.5	27.9	.8	5
1.2	.2	48.3	.5	10
4.0	12.0	8.0	—	515
.8	5.3	3.0	—	132
.7	.5	12.9	4.8	3

Food	Amount	Calories
Guinea hen, flesh and skin	3.5 oz.	158

H

Food	Amount	Calories
Haddock 　fried	3.5 oz.	165
smoked	3.5 oz.	103
Halibut 　broiled	3.5 oz.	171
smoked	3.5 oz.	224
Ham. *See* Pork.		
Hamburger. *See* Beef, hamburger.		
Ham loaf 　home recipe, with salted cracker 　crumbs, eggs	approx. 4 oz.	350
Heart 　Beef, braised	3.5 oz.	188
Chicken, simmered	3.5 oz.	173
Turkey, simmered	3.5 oz.	216
Herring 　Atlantic, raw	3.5 oz.	176

Protein (gr.)	Fat (gr.)	Carbohydrate (gr.)		Sodium (mg)
		Total	Fiber	
23.4	6.4	0	0	—
19.6	6.4	5.8	—	177
23.2	.4	0	0	—
25.2	7.0	0	0	134
20.8	15.0	0	0	—
15.0	20.0	18.0	—	315
31.3	5.7	.7	0	104
25.3	7.2	.1	0	69
22.6	13.2	.2	0	61
17.3	11.3	0	0	—

Food	Amount	Calories
Herring (cont.) Pacific, raw	3.5 oz.	98
Canned, plain	3.5 oz.	208
Pickled, Bismarck type	3.5 oz.	223
Smoked bloaters	3.5 oz.	196
hard	3.5 oz.	300
kippered	3.5 oz.	211
Hickory nuts	1 oz.	192
Hollandaise. *See* Sauces.		
Hominy grits. *See* Corn grits.		
Honey	1 tbs.	64
Horseradish, prepared	1 tbs.	6

I/J

Food	Amount	Calories
Ice cream and frozen custard regular (approx. 10% fat)	½ c.	130

Protein (gr.)	Fat (gr.)	Carbohydrate (gr.)		Sodium (mg)
		Total	Fiber	
17.5	2.6	0	0	74
19.9	13.6	0	0	—
20.4	15.1	0	0	—
19.6	12.4	0	0	—
36.9	15.8	0	0	6231
22.2	12.9	0	0	
3.8	19.6	3.7	.5	—
.1	0	17.4	—	1
.2	trace	1.5	.1	15
3.0	7.1	14.0	0	42

Food	Amount	Calories
Ice cream (cont.) rich (approx. 16% fat)	½ c.	166
Ice milk hard	½ c.	100
soft-serve	½ c.	133
Ices, water Lime	½ c.	111
Pineapple-orange, home recipe, juice only	4 oz.	80
Icing. *See* **Cake icings.**		
Jams and preserves	1 tbs.	55
Jellies	1 tbs.	49
Jerusalem artichoke	3.5 oz.	7–75 (varies fresh to stored)

K/L

Food	Amount	Calories
Kabobs Beef, home recipe, with sweet barbecue sauce, peppers	approx. 5 oz.	360
Lamb, home recipe, with herb sauce, vegetables	approx. 5 oz.	425
Kale cooked	1 c.	31

Protein (gr.)	Fat (gr.)	Carbohydrate (gr.)		Sodium (mg)
		Total	Fiber	
1.9	12.0	13.4	0	25
3.2	3.4	14.8	0	45
4.2	4.5	19.6	0	60
.6	trace	46.6	trace	trace
0	0	20.0	—	1
.1	trace	14.2	.2	2
trace	trace	12.7	0	3
2.3	.1	16.7	.8	—
25.0	25.0	15.0	—	680
20.0	35.0	10.0	—	435
3.5	.8	4.4	1.2	48

Composition of Foods

Food	Amount	Calories
Ketchup. *See* Tomato catsup.		
Kidneys Beef, braised	3.5 oz.	252
Calf, uncooked	3.5 oz.	113
Lamb, uncooked	3.5 oz.	105
Kohlrabi boiled	1 c.	36
Kumquats fresh	3 small	65
Lake herring uncooked	3.5 oz.	96
Lake trout uncooked	3.5 oz.	168
Lamb Leg, choice grade, roasted (83% lean, 17% fat)	3.5 oz.	279
Loin chops, choice grade, broiled (66% lean, 34% fat)	3.5 oz.	359
Rib chops, choice grade, broiled (62% lean, 38% fat)	3.5 oz.	407
Shoulder, choice grade, roasted (74% lean, 26% fat)	3.5 oz.	338
Lard	1 tbs.	119

Protein (gr.)	Fat (gr.)	Carbohydrate (gr.)		Sodium (mg)
		Total	Fiber	
33.0	12.0	.8	0	253
16.6	4.6	.1	0	—
16.8	3.3	.9	0	200
2.6	.2	8.0	1.5	9
.9	11	17.1	3.7	7
17.7	2.3	0	0	47
18.3	10.0	0	0	low
25.3	18.9	0	0	av. 70
22.0	29.4	0	0	av. 70
20.1	35.6	0	0	av. 70
21.7	27.2	0	0	av. 70
0	13.1	0	0	0

Food	Amount	Calories
Lasagna home recipe, with pork sausage or beef, noodles, cheeses	6–7 oz.	630
Leeks raw	3–4	52
Lemonade frozen concentrate, diluted per directions	1 c.	110
Lemon juice fresh	1 c.	61
canned or bottled, unsweetened	1 c.	55
Lemons fresh, peeled	1 med.	27
Lentils whole, cooked	1 c.	214
Lettuce Butterhead varieties	1 head (4″ diam.)	31
Crisp-head varieties	1 head	59
Loose-leafed varieties	2 lg. leaves	7
Limeade concentrate, diluted	1 c.	102
Lime juice fresh, canned, or bottled, unsweetened	1 c.	64

Protein (gr.)	Fat (gr.)	Carbohydrate (gr.)		Sodium (mg)
		Total	Fiber	
30.0	40.0	25.0	—	1330
2.2	.3	11.2	1.3	5
.3	trace	28.5	trace	trace
1.2	.5	19.7	trace	2
1.0	trace	19.0	—	—
1.1	.3	8.2	.4	2
15.7	trace	38.8	2.4	—
2.6	.5	5.5	1.1	20
4.2	.5	13.3	2.2	41
.5	.1	1.5	.2	5
trace	trace	27.3	trace	trace
.8	.3	22.0	trace	3

Food	Amount	Calories
Limes	1 med.	28
Liver Beef, fried	3.5 oz.	229
Calf, fried	3.5 oz.	261
Chicken, simmered	3.5 oz.	165
Goose, uncooked	3.5 oz.	182
Hog, fried	3.5 oz.	241
Lamb, broiled	3.5 oz.	261
Turkey, simmered	3.5 oz.	174
Lobster uncooked, whole	3.5 oz.	91
canned or cooked	3.5 oz.	95
Lobster Newburg	3.5 oz.	194
Lobster salad	3.5 oz.	110
Loganberries fresh	1 c.	83

Protein (gr.)	Fat (gr.)	Carbohydrate (gr.)		Sodium (mg)
		Total	Fiber	
.7	.2	9.5	.5	2
26.4	10.6	5.3	0	184
29.5	13.2	4.0	0	118
26.5	4.4	3.1	0	61
16.5	10.0	5.4	0	140
29.9	11.5	2.5	0	111
32.3	12.4	2.8	0	52
27.9	4.8	3.1	0	55
16.9	1.9	.5	—	high
18.7	1.5	.3	—	210
18.5	10.6	5.1	—	229
10.1	6.4	2.3	—	124
1.4	.8	20.0	4.0	1

Food	Amount	Calories
Loganberries (cont.) canned, juice pack	3.5 oz.	54
Luncheon meats. *See* Sausage, cold cuts, and luncheon meats.		

M

Food	Amount	Calories
Macadamia nuts	1 oz.	197
Macaroni cooked	1 c.	157
Macaroni and cheese baked, home recipe	1 c.	433
canned	1 c.	230
Mackerel Atlantic broiled, with butter	3.5 oz.	236
canned	3.5 oz.	183
Pacific uncooked	3.5 oz.	159
canned	3.5 oz.	180
salted	3.5 oz.	305
smoked	3.5 oz.	219

Protein (gr.)	Fat (gr.)	Carbohydrate (gr.)		Sodium (mg)
		Total	Fiber	
.7	.5	12.7	2.1	1
2.2	20.5	4.5	.7	—
4.8	.5	32.5	.1	1
16.9	22.3	40.5	.2	1094
9.4	9.6	25.9	.3	735
21.8	15.8	0	0	—
19.3	11.1	0	0	—
21.9	7.3	0	0	—
21.1	10.0	0	0	—
18.5	25.1	0	0	—
23.8	13.0	0	0	—

Food	Amount	Calories
Mangoes fresh	1 small	93
Manicotti home recipe, with beef, spinach, cheese	2 filled shells	400
Margarine, corn or vegetable oil, salted	1 tbs.	101
Marmalade	1 tbs.	52
Mayonnaise. *See* Salad dressings.		
Meat loaf home recipe, with ground beef, dry bread crumbs, eggs, milk	4–5 oz.	415
Melons, fresh Cantaloupe	½ melon	116
Casaba	1 wedge	39
Honeydew	½ melon	248
Milk, cow's Canned evaporated, unsweetened	1 c.	348
evaporated skimmed (less than ¼ of 1% butterfat)	4 oz.	100
condensed, sweetened	1 c.	990
Chocolate beverages, homemade hot chocolate	1 c.	239

Protein (gr.)	Fat (gr.)	Carbohydrate (gr.)		Sodium (mg)
		Total	Fiber	
1.0	.6	23.7	1.3	10
30.0	15.0	40.0	—	870
.1	11.3	.1	0	138
1.0	trace	14.2	.1	3
25.0	30.0	15.0	—	650
2.7	.4	29.1	1.2	47
1.7	trace	9.3	.4	17
6.0	2.4	57.8	4.5	90
17.8	20.1	24.6	0	300
9.0	less than 1%	14.0	—	—
24.9	26.9	167.4	0	345
8.3	12.6	26.2	.3	121

Food	Amount	Calories
Milk, chocolate beverages (cont.) hot cocoa	1 c.	244
Chocolate drink, packaged beverage made with skim milk	1 c.	191
made with whole milk (3.5% butterfat)	1 c.	214
Dry whole	1 c.	521
skim, nonfat solids (regular)	1 c.	381
skim, nonfat solids (instant)	1 c.	246
Malted, prepared from powder	1 c.	246
Pasteurized and raw whole (3.5% fat)	1 c.	160
skim	1 c.	89
partially skimmed with 2% nonfat milk added	1 c.	146
See also Buttermilk; Yogurt.		
Milk, goat	1 c.	165
Milk, human	1 c.	139
Milk substitute (infant formula) packaged, ready to use	8 oz.	160

Protein (gr.)	Fat (gr.)	Carbohydrate (gr.)		Sodium (mg)
		Total	Fiber	
9.6	11.6	27.4	.3	129
8.3	5.8	27.4	trace	116
8.6	8.6	27.7	trace	118
27.4	28.5	40.0	0	420
37.7	.7	54.8	0	558
24.6	.5	35.4	0	361
11.1	10.4	27.7	trace	216
8.6	8.6	12.1	0	123
8.9	.3	12.6	0	128
10.4	4.9	14.8	0	151
7.9	9.8	11.3	0	84
2.0	7.2	17.1	0	29
3.6	8.8	16.8	—	52

Food	Amount	Calories
Molasses		
light (1st extraction)	1 tbs.	51
medium (2nd extraction)	1 tbs.	47
blackstrap (3rd extraction)	1 tbs.	43
Muffins, enriched flour		
Home recipe		
Blueberry	1	113
Bran	1	105
Corn (enriched degermed cornmeal)	1	126
English, home recipe, with all-purpose flour, cornmeal, or whole-wheat flour	1	150
Plain	1	118
Made from mix		
with egg, milk	1	131
with egg, water	1	120
Mushrooms		
Cultivated commercially		
raw	4 lg.	28
canned	½ c.	21

Protein (gr.)	Fat (gr.)	Carbohydrate (gr.)		Sodium (mg)
		Total	Fiber	
—	—	13.2	—	3
—	—	12.2	—	8
—	—	11.2	—	19
2.9	3.8	16.9	.1	255
3.1	3.9	17.4	.7	180
2.9	4.1	19.4	.1	194
3.0	4.0	25.0	—	185
3.1	4.1	17.1	trace	178
2.8	4.3	20.1	.1	193
1.8	3.1	20.9	trace	139
2.7	.3	4.4	.8	15
2.3	.1	3.0	.7	491

Food	Amount	Calories
Mushrooms (cont.) Other edible species, raw	½ c.	43
Mussels, Atlantic and Pacific raw	3.5 oz.	95
Mustard, prepared	1 tsp.	5
Mustard greens, cooked	1 c.	32

N/O

Food	Amount	Calories
Nectarines fresh	1 med.	88
Noodles Home recipe, cooked, made with all-purpose flour, egg, milk	½ c.	90
Packaged egg, enriched, cooked	1 c.	201
chow mein, canned	½ c.	110
Nuts. *See* **individual names.**		
Oat products—Packaged, used mainly as hot cereals Oat and wheat cereal	1 c.	157
Oat cereal with toasted wheat germ and soy grits	1 c.	150
Oat flakes, maple-flavored, instant cooking	1 c.	167

Protein (gr.)	Fat (gr.)	Carbohydrate (gr.)		Sodium (mg)
		Total	Fiber	
2.3	.7	8.0	1.4	12
14.4	2.2	3.3	—	289
2.5	.2	.3	.1	64
3.1	.5	5.6	1.3	25
.8	trace	23.5	.5	8
3.0	1.0	16.0	—	190
6.6	2.4	37.6	.2	3
3.0	5.3	13.1	—	—
6.3	2.2	29.2	.7	406
8.0	3.6	23.0	1.5	706
6.3	1.9	31.4	.2	259

Food	Amount	Calories
Oat products (cont.)		
Oat granules, maple-flavored, quick cooking	1 c.	145
Oatmeal or rolled oats, cooked	1 c.	133
Oat products—Packaged, used mainly as ready-to-eat breakfast cereals		
Oats, shredded, with protein and other nutrients	1 c.	96
Oats (with or without corn), puffed, added nutrients	1 c.	100
Oats (with or without corn, wheat), puffed, added nutrients, sugar-coated	1 c.	120
Oats (with soy flour and rice), flaked, added nutrients	1 c.	101
Ocean perch. *See* **Perch.**		
Oils, salad or cooking (corn, olive, peanut, safflower)	1 tbs.	124
Okra cooked	10 pods (3" x 5/8")	31
Olives (pickled), canned or bottled Green	4 med., 3 extra lg., or 2 giant	19
Ripe	3 small or 2 lg.	18
Ascolano and Manzanilla	3.5 oz.	129

Protein (gr.)	Fat (gr.)	Carbohydrate (gr.)		Sodium (mg)
		Total	Fiber	
5.6	1.5	27.6	.5	174
4.8	2.5	23.4	.5	527
4.8	.5	18.0	.5	155
3.0	1.4	18.9	.3	319
2.0	1.0	25.9	.2	178
3.8	1.4	18.0	.2	305
0	14.0	0	0	0
2.1	.3	6.4	1.1	2
.2	2.0	.2	.2	384
.1	2.0	.3	.2	75
1.1	13.8	2.6	1.4	813

Food	Amount	Calories
Olives (cont.) Mission	3.5 oz.	184
Sevillano	3.5 oz.	93
Salt-cured, oil-coated (Greek style)	3.5 oz.	338
Onions Mature raw	1 med.	42
boiled	½ c.	31
Young green raw, bulb and white portion of top	6	14
Onion salt	1 tsp.	—
Orange juice Canned unsweetened	1 c.	120
sweetened	1 c.	130
Frozen concentrate, unsweetened, diluted per directions	1 c.	112
Orange juice, fresh All typical varieties	1 c.	113
California navels (winter)	1 c.	120
California Valencias (summer)	1 c.	117

Protein (gr.)	Fat (gr.)	Carbohydrate (gr.)		Sodium (mg)
		Total	Fiber	
1.2	20.1	3.2	1.5	750
1.1	9.5	2.7	1.2	828
2.2	35.8	8.7	3.8	3288
1.7	.1	9.7	.7	11
1.3	.1	6.9	.6	7
.3	.1	3.2	.3	2
—	—	—	—	1620
2.0	.5	28.1	.3	3
1.8	.5	30.6	.3	3
1.8	.3	26.9	trace	3
1.8	.5	26.0	.2	2
2.5	.2	28.2	.2	2
2.5	.7	26.3	.2	2

Food	Amount	Calories
Orange juice, fresh (cont.)		
Florida (typical varieties)	1 c.	107
temple oranges	1 c.	135
Oranges, fresh, peeled, no seeds		
All typical varieties	1 med.	65
California navels (winter)	1 med.	67
California Valencias (summer)	1 med.	67
Florida (typical varieties)	1 med.	62
Oysters		
Fried	3.5 oz.	239
Canned	3.5 oz.	76
Raw		
Atlantic	1 c.	160
Pacific	1 c.	220
Oyster stew		
Commercial, frozen		
prepared with equal volume of water	1 c.	117
prepared with equal volume of milk	1 c.	192

Protein (gr.)	Fat (gr.)	Carbohydrate (gr.)		Sodium (mg)
		Total	Fiber	
1.5	.5	25.0	.2	2
1.2	.5	32.2	.2	2
1.3	.3	16.1	.6	1
1.7	.1	16.8	.7	1
1.6	.4	16.4	.7	1
.9	.3	15.8	.7	1
8.6	13.9	18.6	trace	206
8.5	2.2	4.9	.1	—
20.3	4.3	8.2	—	176
25.6	5.3	15.5	—	—
5.3	7.3	7.8	trace	777
9.6	11.2	13.5	trace	837

Food	Amount	Calories
Oyster stew (cont.) Home recipe 1 part oysters to 2 parts milk by volume	1 c.	228
1 part oysters to 3 parts milk by volume	1 c. (w/3–4 oysters)	210

P

Pancake and waffle mixes Buckwheat, made with egg, milk	1 cake (4″ diam.)	54
Plain and buttermilk (enriched flour) made with milk	1 cake (4″ diam.)	55
made with egg, milk	1 cake (4″ diam.)	61
Pancakes home recipe (enriched flour)	1 cake (4″ diam.)	63
Papayas fresh, cubes	1 c.	72
Parsley raw, chopped	1 tbs.	2
Parsnips cooked	1 c.	102
Pasta and pasta foods. *See* Fettuccine; Lasagna; Manicotti; Spaghetti. *See also* Macaroni; Noodles; Spaetzle.		
Pastina Carrot	3.5 oz.	371

Protein (gr.)	Fat (gr.)	Carbohydrate (gr.)		Sodium (mg)
		Total	Fiber	
12.2	15.0	10.6	—	797
12.0	12.9	11.5	—	496
1.8	2.5	6.5	.1	126
1.7	1.5	8.7	trace	122
2.0	2.8	8.8	trace	153
1.9	1.9	9.3	trace	115
1.1	.2	18.4	1.7	6
.1	trace	.3	.1	2
2.4	.8	23.2	3.2	12
11.9	1.6	75.7	.6	—

Food	Amount	Calories
Pastina (cont.) Spinach	3.5 oz.	368
Pâté de foie gras	1 tbs.	70
Peaches fresh	1 med.	38
canned, heavy syrup pack	½ c.	101
dried, cooked, unsweetened, solids and liquid	½ c. (5–6 halves)	112
dried, uncooked	1 c.	422
Peanut butter (moderate amounts of fat, sweetener, salt)	1 tbs.	94
Peanuts raw with skins	1 oz.	161
roasted and salted	1 oz.	167
Pears fresh, cored, with skin	1 med.	101
canned, heavy syrup pack	½ c.	98
dried, uncooked	2 halves	108
Peas fresh, boiled, drained	1 c.	114

Protein (gr.)	Fat (gr.)	Carbohydrate (gr.)		Sodium (mg)
		Total	Fiber	
12.4	1.6	74.8	.5	—
1.7	6.6	.7	0	—
.6	.1	9.7	.6	1
.5	.1	26.0	.5	3
1.4	.3	29.1	1.4	7
5.0	1.1	110.1	5.0	26
4.0	8.1	3.0	.3	97
7.4	13.6	5.3	.7	1
7.4	14.2	5.4	.7	119
1.2	.7	25.3	2.3	3
.3	.3	25.2	.8	1
1.2	.7	27.1	2.5	3
8.7	.6	19.5	3.2	2

Food	Amount	Calories
Peas (cont.)		
canned, cooked, solids and liquid	1 c.	166
frozen, cooked	1 c.	155
Peas and carrots		
frozen, cooked	1 c.	80
Pecans, unsalted	1 oz.	196
Peppers, hot chili		
Green, canned	1 c.	49
Red, mature, raw	1 med. (w/o seeds)	65
Peppers, sweet		
raw	1 med.	20
Perch		
Ocean		
Atlantic, fried	3.5 oz.	227
Pacific, raw	3.5 oz.	95
White	3.5 oz.	118
Yellow	3.5 oz.	91
Persimmons	1 small	153
Pheasant, flesh only, uncooked	3.5 oz.	162

Protein (gr.)	Fat (gr.)	Carbohydrate (gr.)		Sodium (mg)
		Total	Fiber	
8.8	.8	31.4	3.8	592
12.0	.7	27.0	4.3	262
4.8	.5	15.2	2.3	127
2.6	20.3	4.2	.7	trace
1.8	.2	12.0	2.4	—
2.3	.4	15.8	2.3	25
1.1	.2	4.4	1.3	12
19.0	13.3	6.8	0	153
19.0	1.5	0	0	63
19.3	4.0	0	0	—
19.5	.9	0	0	68
1.0	.5	40.5	1.8	1
23.6	6.8	0	0	—

Food	Amount	Calories
Pickerel, chain raw	3.5 oz.	84
Pickle relish, sweet, finely chopped	1 tbs.	21
Pickles Bread-and-butter	2 slices (1½" x ¼")	10
Dill	1 med.	7
Sweet, gherkin	1 small (2½" x ¾")	20
Pies	1/7 of a 9" pie	
Apple	1 piece	348
Banana custard	1 piece	290
Blackberry	1 piece	330
Blueberry	1 piece	329
Boston cream. *See* Cakes.		
Butterscotch	1 piece	350
Cherry	1 piece	355

Protein (gr.)	Fat (gr.)	Carbohydrate (gr.)		Sodium (mg)
		Total	Fiber	
18.7	.5	0	0	—
.1	.1	5.1	.1	108
trace	trace	3.0	—	101
.5	.1	1.4	.3	934
trace	trace	5.0	—	128
3.0	15.1	51.8	.5	409
5.9	12.2	40.3	.3	254
3.5	15.0	46.8	2.6	364
3.3	14.7	47.5	1.0	364
5.8	14.4	50.2	trace	281
3.5	15.4	52.2	.1	413

Food	Amount	Calories
Pies (cont.)		
Chocolate chiffon	1 piece	307
Chocolate meringue	1 piece	305
Coconut custard	1 piece	308
Custard	1 piece	286
Lemon chiffon	1 piece	293
Lemon meringue	1 piece	308
Mince	1 piece	369
Peach	1 piece	288
Pecan	1 piece	497
Pineapple	1 piece	344
Pineapple chiffon	1 piece	270
Pineapple custard	1 piece	289
Pumpkin	1 piece	277

Protein (gr.)	Fat (gr.)	Carbohydrate (gr.)		Sodium (mg)
		Total	Fiber	
6.4	14.3	41.0	.2	236
5.8	14.5	40.5	.2	309
7.9	16.4	32.7	.3	324
8.0	14.6	30.1	trace	376
6.6	11.8	41.0	trace	245
4.5	12.3	45.6	trace	341
3.4	15.6	56.0	.5	609
2.8	12.1	43.1	.5	302
6.1	27.2	61.0	.6	263
3.0	14.6	51.8	.3	369
6.2	11.3	36.6	.1	240
5.2	11.4	42.1	.1	244
5.2	14.7	32.1	.7	281

Food	Amount	Calories
Pies (cont.) Raisin	1 piece	340
Rhubarb	1 piece	264
Strawberry	1 piece	269
Pigs' feet, pickled	3.5 oz.	199
Pike Blue, raw	3.5 oz.	90
Northern, raw	3.5 oz.	88
Walleye, raw	3.5 oz.	93
Pimientos	1 med.	10
Pineapple fresh, diced	1 c.	73
canned, heavy syrup, slices and juice	2 small slices or 1 lg. slice	91
canned, heavy syrup, all other styles	½ c.	95
Pineapple and grapefruit juice drink canned	1 c.	136
Pineapple and orange juice drink canned	1 c.	136

Protein (gr.)	Fat (gr.)	Carbohydrate (gr.)		Sodium (mg)
		Total	Fiber	
3.3	13.5	54.2	.4	359
2.6	11.2	39.8	.6	282
2.6	10.7	42.0	1.1	264
16.7	14.8	0	0	—
19.1	.9	0	0	—
18.3	1.1	0	0	—
19.3	1.2	0	0	51
.3	.2	2.2	.2	—
.6	.3	19.3	.6	1
.4	trace	23.8	.4	1
.4	trace	24.9	.4	1
.5	trace	34.3	trace	trace
.5	.3	34.0	trace	trace

Food	Amount	Calories
Pineapple juice canned, unsweetened	1 c.	139
Pistachio nuts	1 oz.	170
Pita bread Home recipe, with all-purpose flour, salt	1 (5–6" round)	160
Packaged regular size	1 (approx. 2 oz.)	165
small size	1 (approx. 1 oz.)	70
Pizza, baked	⅙ of a 12" pie	
with cheese	1 slice	143
with sausage	1 slice	175
Plate Dinners—Frozen, packaged Beef pot roast with roasted potatoes, peas and corn	3.5 oz.	106
Chicken, fried, with mashed potatoes, mixed vegetables	3.5 oz.	173
Meatloaf with tomato sauce, mashed potatoes, peas	3.5 oz.	131
Turkey, sliced, with mashed potatoes, peas	3.5 oz.	112

Protein (gr.)	Fat (gr.)	Carbohydrate (gr.)		Sodium (mg)
		Total	Fiber	
1.0	.3	33.0	.26	2.5
5.5	15.3	5.4	.5	low
4.0	5.0	25.0	—	270
6.0	trace	34.0	—	—
4.0	1.5	14.0	—	—
7.3	5.0	17.1	.2	425
5.8	7.0	22.2	.2	546
13.1	3.2	6.1	.3	259
12.8	8.5	11.3	.4	344
8.0	6.7	9.8	.3	393
8.4	3.0	12.7	.3	400

Food	Amount	Calories
Plums fresh	1 med.	32
canned, heavy syrup	½ c.	108
Pollack creamed, cooked	3.5 oz.	128
Pomegranates fresh	1 med.	75
Popcorn, popped plain	1 c.	23
with oil and salt	1 c.	42
sugar-coated, without added salt	1 c.	135
Popovers	1 med.	100
Popsicle	1 (3 fl. oz.)	70
Pork, cured Boston butt, light cure, roasted (83% lean, 17% fat)	3.5 oz.	330
Ham, canned	3.5 oz.	193
Ham, light cure, total edible, roasted (84% lean, 16% fat)	3.5 oz.	289
Ham, long cure, country style	3.5 oz.	389

Protein (gr.)	Fat (gr.)	Carbohydrate (gr.)		Sodium (mg)
		Total	Fiber	
.3	.1	8.2	.4	1
.5	.1	28.0	.4	1
13.9	5.9	4.0	—	111
.6	.4	19.5	.2	4
.8	.3	4.6	.1	trace
.9	2.0	5.4	.2	177
2.1	1.2	30.0	.4	trace
3.9	4.1	11.5	trace	98
0	0	18.0	0	—
22.9	25.7	0	0	very high
18.3	12.3	.9	0	1100
20.9	22.1	0	0	very high
16.9	35.0	.3	0	very high

Food	Amount	Calories
Pork, cured (cont.) Picnic, light cure, roasted (82% lean, 18% fat)	3.5 oz.	323
Pork, fresh Boston butt, roasted (79% lean, 21% fat)	3.5 oz.	353
Ham, roasted (74% lean, 26% fat)	3.5 oz.	374
Loin, roasted (80% lean, 20% fat)	3.5 oz.	362
Picnic, simmered (74% lean, 26% fat)	3.5 oz.	374
Spareribs, braised	3.5 oz.	440
Pork and beans, canned. *See* **Beans, common.**		
Pork and gravy canned (90% pork, 10% gravy)	3.5 oz.	256
Potato chips	10 chips (2″ diam.)	115
Potatoes, white Raw	1 med. (3 per lb.)	116
diced	1 c.	169
Cooked au gratin or scalloped with cheese	1 c.	358

Protein (gr.)	Fat (gr.)	Carbohydrate (gr.)		Sodium (mg)
		Total	Fiber	
22.4	25.2	0	0	very high
22.5	28.5	0	0	65 av. per 100 mg of cooked meat
23.0	30.6	0	0	65 av. per 100 mg of cooked meat
24.5	28.5	0	0	65 av. per 100 mg of cooked meat
23.2	30.5	0	0	65 av. per 100 mg of cooked meat
20.8	38.9	0	0	65 av. per 100 mg of cooked meat
16.4	17.8	6.3	0	—
1.1	8.1	10.1	.3	203
3.2	.2	26.0	.8	5
4.7	.2	38.1	1.1	7
13.1	19.5	33.6	.7	1103

Food	Amount	Calories
Potatoes (cont.) baked in skin, without salt	1 med. (3 per lb.)	142
boiled in skin, without salt	1 med. (3 per lb.)	116
French fried, without salt	10 pieces	157
fried from raw	1 c.	480
home fried (from cooked) in bacon drippings or oil	1 c.	230
mashed with milk and butter	1 c.	199
Canned, with salt added	1 c.	111
Dehydrated mashed (flakes), made with water, milk, and butter	1 c.	197
Frozen French fried, heated, with salt added	10 pieces	126
hashbrowns	1 c.	350
Potato salad home recipe with cooked salad dressing	1 c.	249
Pretzels	1 oz.	111
Dutch	1 (2¾" x 2⅝")	60

Protein (gr.)	Fat (gr.)	Carbohydrate (gr.)		Sodium (mg)
		Total	Fiber	
4.0	.2	32.1	.9	6
3.2	.2	26.0	.8	5
2.5	7.5	20.6	.6	3
7.2	25.4	58.4	1.8	399
6.0	14.0	45.0	—	540
4.4	9.1	26.0	.8	701
2.8	.5	24.7	.5	753
4.0	6.8	30.7	.6	489
2.1	4.8	.6	.4	216
3.1	18.0	45.3	1.1	467
6.8	7.1	41.1	1.0	1331
2.8	1.3	21.7	.1	480
2.0	1.0	12.0	—	270

Food	Amount	Calories
Pretzels (cont.) Soft, home recipe, with salt, yeast	1 (6–8")	160
Stick	10 (ea. 2¼")	10
Prune juice	1 c.	199
Prunes dried, softened, uncooked	4 extra lg. or 5 lg.	111
dried, cooked, no sugar added	1 c.	255
Prune whip	½ c.	100
Puddings, starch-based *Home recipe* Chocolate	½ c.	195
Vanilla	½ c.	143
Made from mix Chocolate, cooked with milk	approx. ½ c.	124
Chocolate, instant, with milk	approx. ½ c.	125
See also Bread pudding; Rice pudding; Tapioca desserts.		
Pumpkin, canned, without salt	1 c.	76
Pumpkin and squash seed kernels	1 oz.	158

Protein (gr.)	Fat (gr.)	Carbohydrate (gr.)		Sodium (mg)
		Total	Fiber	
4.0	3.0	30.0	—	2275
trace	trace	2	—	50
1.0	.3	49.0	trace	5
.9	.3	29.3	.7	3
2.1	.6	67.4	1.7	9
2.8	.1	23.6	.4	105
4.1	6.2	33.8	.3	74
4.5	5.0	20.4	trace	84
3.4	3.0	22.8	.1	129
3.0	2.5	24.4	.1	124
2.3	.7	18.1	3.0	5
8.3	13.3	4.3	.5	—

Food	Amount	Calories

Q/R

Food	Amount	Calories
Quail flesh and skin, uncooked	3.5 oz.	172
Quiche *Home recipe* Lorraine, made with bacon, Swiss cheese, eggs, milk, light cream, salt, in pie shell	1/6 of a 9" pie	545
Salmon or tuna, filling only, made with Swiss cheese, eggs, milk, salt	approx. 4 oz.	285
Made from mix filling only	approx. 4 oz.	230
Quinces fresh	1 med.	21
Rabbit, domestic stewed	3.5 oz.	216
Radishes	4 small	7
Raisins uncooked	1 c. pressed down	481
Raspberries Black, fresh	1 c.	90
Red fresh	1 c.	70
frozen, sweetened	10 oz. pkg.	280

Protein (gr.)	Fat (gr.)	Carbohydrate (gr.)		Sodium (mg)
		Total	Fiber	
25.4	7.0	0	0	40
20.0	40.0	25.0	—	745
28.0	20.0	8.0	—	770
13.0	18.0	4.0	—	385
.1	trace	5.7	.6	1
29.3	10.1	0	0	41
.4	trace	1.5	.3	7
4.2	.3	128.7	1.5	45
1.8	1.7	19.3	6.3	1
1.5	.6	16.7	3.7	1
2.0	.6	70.3	6.3	3

Food	Amount	Calories
Relish. *See* Pickle relish.		
Rhubarb uncooked	1 c.	20
fresh, cooked, added sugar	½ c.	193
frozen, cooked, added sugar	½ c.	196
Rice Brown, boiled	1 c.	234
White, enriched, regular, boiled	1 c.	225
Instant	1 c.	181
See also Wild rice.		
Rice products, granulated—Packaged, used mainly as hot breakfast cereal, cooked	1 c.	123
Rice products, puffed—Packaged, used mainly as ready-to-eat breakfast cereal plain puffed rice, without salt	1 c.	60
presweetened, with honey or cocoa, added nutrients including fat	1 c.	115

Protein (gr.)	Fat (gr.)	Carbohydrate (gr.)		Sodium (mg)
		Total	Fiber	
.8	.1	1.3	.9	3
.7	.1	49.4	.8	3
.7	.3	49.6	1.1	4
4.9	1.2	50.1	.6	554
4.1	.2	50.0	.2	773
3.7	trace	40.2	.2	454
2.0	trace	27.6	trace	434
.9	.1	13.6	.1	.3
1.3	1.1	24.8	.1	102

Food	Amount	Calories
Rice pudding with raisins	½ c.	191
Rolls and buns *Home recipe* Hot-cross buns	1	235
Plain rolls	1	119
Packaged Brown-and-serve-type rolls, browned	1	87
Danish pastry	1 round	276
Frankfurter and hamburger rolls	1	120
Hard rolls, enriched	1	157
Pan rolls, plain, enriched	1 (2½" x 2")	85
Raisin rolls or buns	1	118
Sweet rolls	1 lg.	181
Whole-wheat rolls	1	104
Rutabagas boiled	1 c.	71

Protein (gr.)	Fat (gr.)	Carbohydrate (gr.)		Sodium (mg)
		Total	Fiber	
4.7	4.1	35.0	.1	93
5.0	8.0	38.0	—	110
2.9	3.1	19.7	.1	98
2.3	2.0	14.4	.1	148
4.8	15.4	29.8	.1	239
3.0	2.0	21.0	—	moderate to high
4.9	1.6	29.9	.1	314
2.3	1.6	15.1	.1	145
3.0	1.2	24.2	.4	165
4.9	5.2	28.2	.1	222
4.0	1.1	21.1	.6	227
1.8	.2	16.5	2.2	8

Food	Amount	Calories

S

Food	Amount	Calories
Salad dressings *Home recipe* Cooked	1 tbs.	26
French	1 tbs.	88
Italian, with Parmesan cheese, sugar, salt	1 oz.	190
Vinaigrette, with sugar, salt	1 oz.	165
Prepared Blue and Roquefort regular	1 tbs.	76
low calorie	1 tbs.	12
French regular	1 tbs.	66
low calorie	1 tbs.	15
Italian regular	1 tbs.	84
low calorie	1 tbs.	8
Mayonnaise regular	1 tbs.	101
reduced calorie	1 tbs.	40

Protein (gr.)	Fat (gr.)	Carbohydrate (gr.)		Sodium (mg)
		Total	Fiber	
.7	1.6	2.4	0	116
trace	9.8	.5	trace	92
0	21.0	1.0	—	410
0	18.0	1.0	—	270
.7	7.9	1.1	trace	166
.5	.9	.6	trace	168
.1	6.2	2.8	trace	219
.1	.7	2.4	trace	119
trace	9.1	1.0	trace	317
trace	.7	.4	trace	119
.2	11.2	.3	trace	84
0	4.0	1.0	—	—

Food	Amount	Calories
Salad dressings, prepared (cont.) Russian	1 tbs.	75
Thousand Island regular	1 tbs.	80
low calorie	1 tbs.	27
Salmon, canned Atlantic	3.5 oz.	203
Chinook (king), without salt	3.5 oz.	210
Chum, without salt	3.5 oz.	139
Coho (silver)	3.5 oz.	153
Pink (humpback)	3.5 oz.	141
Sockeye (red)	3.5 oz.	171
Salmon, fresh broiled or baked	3.5 oz.	182
Salmon, smoked	3.5 oz.	176
Salmon loaf home recipe, with egg, milk, bread crumbs	4–5 oz.	340

Protein (gr.)	Fat (gr.)	Carbohydrate (gr.)		Sodium (mg)
		Total	Fiber	
.2	7.7	1.6	trace	131
.1	8.0	2.5	trace	112
.1	2.1	2.4	trace	106
21.7	12.2	0	0	—
19.6	14.0	0	0	45
21.5	5.2	0	0	53
20.8	7.1	0	0	351 w/salt, 48 w/o salt
20.5	5.9	0	0	387 w/salt, 64 w/o salt
20.3	9.3	0	0	522 w/salt, 48 w/o salt
27.0	7.4	0	0	116
21.6	9.3	0	0	—
30.0	15.0	20.0	—	1060

Food	Amount	Calories
Salt, table	1 tsp.	0
Salt pork uncooked	3.5 oz.	783
Salt sticks regular	1 oz.	110
Vienna-bread type	1 oz.	87
Sandwich spread with chopped pickle regular	1 oz.	108
low calorie	1 oz.	32
Sardines Atlantic, canned in oil, drained	3.5 oz.	203
Pacific, canned in brine or mustard, solids and liquid	3.5 oz.	196
Pacific, canned in tomato sauce, solids and liquid	3.5 oz.	197
Sauces, home recipe Béarnaise, with egg yolks, butter	1 oz.	256
Bordelaise, with butter, beef broth, cornstarch, red wine	2 oz.	35
Hollandaise, with egg yolks, butter, salt	1 oz.	130

Protein (gr.)	Fat (gr.)	Carbohydrate (gr.)		Sodium (mg)
		Total	Fiber	
0	0	0	0	1993
3.9	85.0	0	0	1212
3.4	.8	21.5	.1	478
2.7	.9	16.6	.1	447
.2	10.3	4.5	.1	179
.3	2.6	2.3	.1	179
24.0	11.1	—	—	823
18.8	12.0	1.7	—	760
18.7	12.2	1.7	—	400
3.0	28.0	1.0	—	290
0	1.0	3.0	—	140
1.0	14.0	0	0	145

Food	Amount	Calories
Sauces (cont.) White, medium, with enriched flour	½ c.	204
See also Barbecue sauce.		
Sauerbraten home recipe, marinated, with gingersnaps, without noodles	4–5 oz.	655
Sauerkraut canned, solids and liquid	1 c.	43
Sausage, cold cuts, and luncheon meats Blood sausage or blood pudding	1 oz.	113
Bockwurst	1 oz.	75
Boiled ham	1 oz.	67
Bologna, all meat	1 oz.	79
Bratwurst	1 oz.	—
Braunschweiger	1 oz.	91
Brown-and-serve-type sausage, browned	1 oz.	121
Capocollo	1 oz.	143

Protein (gr.)	Fat (gr.)	Carbohydrate (gr.)		Sodium (mg)
		Total	Fiber	
4.9	15.7	11.1	trace	478
30.0	45.0	35.0	—	730
2.4	.5	9.5	1.7	1769
4.0	10.5	.1	0	—
3.2	6.8	.2	0	—
5.4	4.9	0	0	—
3.8	6.5	1.1	0	high
—	—	—	—	158
4.2	7.8	.7	—	high
4.7	10.8	.8	0	high
5.8	13.1	0	0	—

Food	Amount	Calories
Sausage, etc. (cont.) Cervelat, soft	1 oz.	88
Country-style sausage	1 oz.	99
Deviled ham, canned	1 oz.	100
Frankfurters, all meat, uncooked	1 med.	169
Headcheese	1 oz.	77
Knockwurst	1 oz.	79
Liverwurst, fresh	1 oz.	88
Meat, potted	1 oz.	71
Minced ham	1 oz.	65
Mortadella	1 oz.	90
Polish-style sausage	1 oz.	87
Pork sausage links or bulk, cooked	1 oz.	136
canned, drained	1 oz.	109
Salami cooked	1 oz.	89

Protein (gr.)	Fat (gr.)	Carbohydrate (gr.)		Sodium (mg)
		Total	Fiber	
5.3	7.0	.5	0	high
4.3	8.9	0	0	—
4.0	9.2	0	0	253
7.5	14.6	1.4	0	639
4.4	6.3	.3	0	high
4.0	6.6	.6	0	very high
4.6	7.3	.5	0	—
5.0	5.5	0	0	—
3.9	4.8	1.3	0	—
5.8	7.1	.2	0	—
4.5	7.4	.3	0	high
5.2	12.6	trace	0	274
5.2	9.4	.5	0	—
5.0	7.3	.4	0	high

Food	Amount	Calories
Sausage, etc., Salami (cont.) dry	1 oz.	129
Scrapple	1 oz.	61
Vienna sausage, canned	1	38
Scallops steamed	3.5 oz.	112
frozen, breaded, fried	3.5 oz.	194
Sea bass, white uncooked	3.5 oz.	96
Sesame seeds dried	1 oz.	166
Shad baked with butter and bacon	3.5 oz.	201
Creole, prepared with tomato, onion, green pepper, flour, and butter	3.5 oz.	152
Shallots	1 bulb	15
Sherbet, orange	½ c.	130
Shish kebab. *See* **Kabobs.**		

Protein (gr.)	Fat (gr.)	Carbohydrate (gr.)		Sodium (mg)
		Total	Fiber	
6.8	10.9	.3	0	high
2.5	3.9	4.1	trace	—
2.2	—	—	0	152
23.2	1.4	—	—	265
18.0	8.4	10.5	—	very high
21.4	.5	0	0	low
5.2	15.3	5.0	.7	—
23.2	11.3	0	0	79
15.0	8.7	1.6	—	73
.5	trace	3.4	.1	3
.9	1.2	29.9	0	10

Food	Amount	Calories
Shrimp uncooked	3.5 oz.	91
French fried, dipped in egg, crumbs, and flour	3.5 oz.	225
canned, dry pack or wet pack drained	3.5 oz.	116
Snapper, red or gray	3.5 oz.	93
Soda. *See* Beverages.		
Soups, canned Asparagus, cream of with water	1 c.	65
with milk	1 c.	148
Bean with pork, with water	1 c.	169
Beef broth, bouillon, and consommé, with water	1 c.	31
Beef noodle, with water	1 c.	68
Celery, cream of with water	1 c.	87
with milk	1 c.	170

Protein (gr.)	Fat (gr.)	Carbohydrate (gr.)		Sodium (mg)
		Total	Fiber	
18.1	.8	1.5	—	140
20.3	10.8	10.0	—	186
24.2	1.1	.7	—	—
19.8	.9	0	0	67
2.4	1.7	10.2	.7	991
6.9	5.9	16.8	.7	1076
8.1	5.8	21.9	1.5	1016
5.1	0	2.7	trace	788
3.9	2.7	7.0	trace	923
1.7	5.1	8.9	.5	962
6.4	9.4	15.3	.5	1047

Food	Amount	Calories
Soups, canned (cont.) Chicken, cream of with water	1 c.	94
with milk	1 c.	180
Chicken consommé, with water	1 c.	22
Chicken gumbo, with water	1 c.	56
Chicken noodle, with water	1 c.	63
Chicken vegetable, with water	1 c.	77
Chicken with rice, with water	1 c.	48
Clam chowder, Manhattan type (with tomatoes, no milk), with water	1 c.	81
Minestrone, with water	1 c.	106
Mushroom, cream of with water	1 c.	135
with milk	1 c.	217
Onion, with water	1 c.	65

Protein (gr.)	Fat (gr.)	Carbohydrate (gr.)		Sodium (mg)
		Total	Fiber	
2.9	5.8	8.0	.2	977
7.4	10.4	14.6	.2	1061
3.4	trace	1.9	trace	728
3.1	1.5	7.5	.2	957
3.4	1.9	8.0	.2	986
4.2	2.5	9.6	.2	1042
3.1	1.2	5.8	trace	923
2.2	2.5	12.3	.5	945
4.9	3.5	14.3	.7	1002
2.4	9.7	10.2	.2	962
6.9	14.3	16.3	.2	1047
5.3	2.4	5.3	.5	1059

Food	Amount	Calories
Soups, canned (cont.) Pea, green with water	1 c.	131
with milk	1 c.	214
Split pea, with water	1 c.	146
Tomato with water	1 c.	89
with milk	1 c.	174
Turkey noodle, with water	1 c.	80
Vegetable beef, with water	1 c.	79
Vegetable with beef broth, with water	1 c.	79
Vegetarian vegetable, with water	1 c.	79
Soups, dehydrated, packaged, prepared with water Beef noodle	1 c.	68
Chicken noodle	1 c.	53
Chicken rice	1 c.	48

Protein (gr.)	Fat (gr.)	Carbohydrate (gr.)		Sodium (mg)
		Total	Fiber	
5.7	2.2	22.7	1.0	906
10.6	6.6	29.5	1.0	990
8.6	3.2	20.7	.5	272
2.0	2.5	15.8	.5	978
6.6	7.1	22.7	.5	1063
4.4	2.9	8.5	.2	1006
5.2	2.2	9.6	.5	1054
2.7	1.7	13.6	.7	852
2.2	2.0	13.3	.5	844
2.4	1.2	11.6	trace	423
1.9	1.5	7.7	trace	583
1.2	1.0	8.5	trace	626

Food	Amount	Calories
Soups, dehydrated (cont.) Onion	1 c.	36
Pea, green	1 c.	123
Tomato vegetable with noodles	1 c.	65
Soups, frozen Clam chowder, New England type (with milk, no tomatoes) with water	1 c.	131
with milk	1 c.	212
Pea, green, with ham	1 c.	141
Potato, cream of with water	1 c.	106
with milk	1 c.	188
Shrimp, cream of with water	1 c.	160
with milk	1 c.	244
Vegetable with beef, with water	1 c.	86
Soups, home recipe Beef barley, with salt added	approx. 1 c.	345

Protein (gr.)	Fat (gr.)	Carbohydrate (gr.)		Sodium (mg)
		Total	Fiber	
1.5	1.2	5.6	.2	694
7.7	1.5	20.7	.5	802
1.5	1.5	12.3	.2	1032
4.4	7.7	10.6	.2	1051
9.1	12.3	16.5	.2	1138
9.4	3.0	19.7	1.7	926
3.4	5.3	11.8	.5	1184
7.9	9.6	18.5	.5	1274
4.8	12.1	8.5	.5	1039
9.3	16.5	15.3	.5	1126
6.7	3.0	8.4	.5	978
20.0	21.0	21.0	—	930

Food	Amount	Calories
Soups, home recipe (cont.) Chicken vegetable, with salt added	1 serv.	300
Lentil, with bacon, vegetables, salt added	1 c.	250
Minestrone, with bacon, noodles, beans, vegetables, salt added	1 c.	255
Mushroom, cream of, with butter, milk, salt added	5 oz.	160
Onion, with condensed beef broth, butter, bread, cheese	4–5 oz.	285
Split pea, with ham bone and meat, onion	approx. 1 c.	235
Vichyssoise, with butter, milk, cream, chicken broth, salt added	6–8 oz.	420
Sour cream	1 tbs.	25
Sourdough bread. *See* Breads.		
Soybean curd (tofu)	1 cake (2½" x 1¾" x 2")	82
Soybeans Fermented (miso), with cereal	3.5 oz.	171
Mature seeds, dry raw	1 c.	702
cooked, without salt	1 c.	260

Protein (gr.)	Fat (gr.)	Carbohydrate (gr.)		Sodium (mg)
		Total	Fiber	
35.0	10.0	20.0	—	660
15.0	5.0	40.0	—	800
12.0	6.0	40.0	—	695
5.0	10.0	12.0	—	560
12.0	12.0	35.0	—	1515
15.0	6.0	30.0	—	295
10.0	35.0	30.0	—	920
trace	3.0	1.0	0	6
8.9	4.8	2.7	.1	8
10.5	4.6	23.5	2.3	2950
59.4	30.8	58.4	8.5	9
22.0	11.4	21.6	3.2	4

Food	Amount	Calories
Soybeans (cont.)		
Immature seeds, canned, solids and liquid	1 c.	150
Sprouted seeds, raw	1 c.	49
Soy sauce	1 tbs.	12
Spaetzle home recipe, with all-purpose flour, eggs, milk, butter, bread crumbs	½ c.	224
Spaghetti, enriched, packaged firm stage, al dente (8–10 minutes)	1 c.	195
tender stage (14–20 minutes)	1 c.	157
Spaghetti in tomato sauce with cheese home recipe	1 c.	262
canned	1 c.	192
Spaghetti with meatballs in tomato sauce home recipe	1 c.	335
canned	1 c.	260
Spanish rice with tomatoes home recipe	1 c.	219

Protein (gr.)	Fat (gr.)	Carbohydrate (gr.)		Sodium (mg)
		Total	Fiber	
13.0	6.4	12.6	1.4	472
6.6	1.5	5.6	.8	—
1.0	.2	1.7	0	1318
7.0	9.0	30.0	—	410
6.6	.7	39.6	.1	1
4.8	.6	32.5	.1	1
8.8	8.8	37.3	.5	963
5.5	1.5	38.8	.5	963
18.7	11.7	40.0	.7	1016
12.3	10.3	28.7	.3	1230
4.5	4.3	41.8	1.3	796

Food	Amount	Calories
Spinach raw, chopped	1 c.	14
cooked	1 c.	42
canned, drained	1 c.	50
frozen leaf, boiled, drained	1 c.	46
Squash, frozen, cooked Summer, yellow crookneck	1 c.	42
Winter	1 c.	76
Squash, summer All types, raw	1 med.	19
Crookneck and straightneck, yellow, cooked	1 c.	32
Scallop varieties, white and pale green, cooked	1 c.	34
Zucchini and cocozelle, green, cooked	1 c.	25
Squash, winter Acorn baked	½ med. squash	86
boiled	1 c.	70

Protein (gr.)	Fat (gr.)	Carbohydrate (gr.)		Sodium (mg)
		Total	Fiber	
1.8	.2	2.4	.3	40
5.4	.5	6.5	1.1	91
5.6	1.2	7.4	1.9	488
5.6	.6	7.5	1.5	94
2.8	.2	9.4	1.2	6
2.4	.6	18.4	2.4	2
1.1	.1	4.2	.6	1
2.1	.4	6.6	1.3	2
1.5	.2	8.0	1.3	2
2.1	.2	5.3	1.3	2
3.0	.2	21.9	2.8	2
2.5	.2	17.4	2.9	2

Food	Amount	Calories
Squash, winter (cont.) Butternut baked	1 c.	140
boiled	1 c.	85
Hubbard baked	1 c.	103
boiled	1 c.	62
Steak. *See* Beef.		
Strawberries fresh	1 c.	56
frozen, sliced, sweetened	½ c.	140
Strawberry shortcake home recipe, with cake, berries, whipped cream	⅛ of an 8″ cake	457
Stuffing. *See* Bread stuffing.		
Sturgeon cooked	3.5 oz.	160
smoked	3.5 oz.	149
Sugar Beet or cane brown	1 tsp.	17

Protein (gr.)	Fat (gr.)	Carbohydrate (gr.)		Sodium (mg)
		Total	Fiber	
3.7	.2	36.2	3.7	2
2.3	.2	21.5	2.9	2
3.7	.8	24.2	3.7	2
2.3	.6	14.3	2.9	2
1.1	.8	12.7	2.0	2
.6	.3	35.7	1.0	1
6.0	27.0	48.0	—	480
25.4	5.7	0	0	108
31.2	1.8	0	0	—
0	0	4.4	0	1

Food	Amount	Calories
Sugar (cont.) granulated	1 tsp.	17
powdered	1 tsp.	10
Maple	1 oz. (1¾" x 1¼" x½" piece)	99
Sunflower seed kernels, dried	1 oz.	160
Sweetbreads (thymus) Beef (yearlings)	3.5 oz.	320
Calf	3.5 oz.	168
Lamb	3.5 oz.	175
Sweet potatoes baked in skin, peeled	1 med.	161
boiled in skin, peeled	1 med.	173
candied	1 med.	296
Swordfish broiled with butter	3.5 oz.	174
Syrup Cane	1 tbs.	56
Maple	1 tbs.	53

Protein (gr.)	Fat (gr.)	Carbohydrate (gr.)		Sodium (mg)
		Total	Fiber	
0	0	4.3	0	trace
0	0	2.6	0	trace
—	—	25.7	—	4
6.9	13.5	5.7	1.1	9
25.9	23.2	0	0	116
32.6	3.2	0	0	moderate
28.1	6.1	0	0	—
2.4	.6	37.1	1.0	14
2.6	.6	39.8	1.1	15
2.3	5.8	60.3	1.1	74
28.0	6.0	0	0	—
0	0	14.4	0	—
—	—	13.7	—	2

Food	Amount	Calories
Syrup (cont.) Sorghum	1 tbs.	54
Table blends cane and maple	1 tbs.	53
chiefly corn, light and dark	1 tbs.	61

T

Food	Amount	Calories
Tangerine juice canned, unsweetened	1 c.	108
canned, sweetened	1 c.	125
frozen concentrate, diluted	1 c.	115
Tangerines raw	1 med.	40
Tapioca desserts Apple tapioca	½ c.	147
Tapioca cream pudding	½ c.	111
Tartar sauce regular	1 tbs.	74
low calorie	1 tbs.	30
Tea, instant powder prepared with water	1 c.	5

Protein (gr.)	Fat (gr.)	Carbohydrate (gr.)		Sodium (mg)
		Total	Fiber	
—	—	14.4	—	—
0	0	13.7	0	trace
0	0	15.9	0	14
1.3	.5	25.6	.3	3
1.3	.5	30.1	.3	3
1.3	.5	27.1	.3	3
.7	.2	10.0	.4	2
.3	.1	37.0	.1	64
4.2	4.2	14.2	0	130
.2	8.1	.6	trace	99
.1	3.0	.9	trace	95
—	trace	.9	trace	low

Food	Amount	Calories
Three-bean salad home recipe, marinated in salad oil and vinegar, with sugar added	approx. ½ c.	270
Tofu. *See* **Soybean curd.**		
Tomato, stuffed home recipe, with tuna, cheese, olives	1 med. tomato, 2 oz. tuna	225
Tomato catsup bottled	1 tbs.	18
Tomato chili sauce	1 tbs.	18
Tomatoes, ripe raw	1 med.	30
boiled	1 c.	63
canned, regular pack	1 c.	51
Tomato juice regular, canned or bottled	1 c.	46
concentrate, diluted per directions	1 c.	48
Tomato juice cocktail canned or bottled	1 c.	51
Tomato paste canned	1 tbs.	13

Protein (gr.)	Fat (gr.)	Carbohydrate (gr.)		Sodium (mg)
		Total	Fiber	
5.0	20.0	25.0	—	120
20.0	8.0	19.0	—	865
.3	.1	4.4	.1	179
.4	.1	4.3	.1	229
1.5	.3	6.4	.7	4
3.2	.5	13.4	1.5	10
2.4	.5	10.4	1.0	316
2.2	.2	10.4	.5	483
2.2	.2	10.9	.5	505
1.7	.2	12.1	.5	483
.6	.1	3.0	.1	6

Food	Amount	Calories
Tomato purée canned	1 tbs.	6
Tongue, braised Beef	3.5 oz.	244
Calf	3.5 oz.	160
Tongue, canned or cured whole, canned or pickled	3.5 oz.	267
potted or deviled	1 oz.	83
smoked (beef)	3.5 oz.	—
Tripe	3.5 oz.	100
pickled	3.5 oz.	62
Trout Brook uncooked	3.5 oz.	101
Rainbow uncooked	3.5 oz.	195
canned	3.5 oz.	209
See also Lake trout.		
Tuna, canned in oil, drained	3.5 oz.	197

Protein (gr.)	Fat (gr.)	Carbohydrate (gr.)		Sodium (mg)
		Total	Fiber	
.3	trace	1.4	.1	63
21.5	16.7	.4	0	61
23.9	6.0	1.0	0	—
19.3	20.3	.3	0	—
5.3	6.6	.2	0	—
17.2	—	0	0	—
19.1	2.0	0	0	72
11.8	1.3	0	0	46
19.2	2.1	0	0	—
21.5	11.4	0	0	—
20.6	13.4	0	0	—
28.8	8.2	0	0	moderate to high

Food	Amount	Calories
Tuna, canned (cont.) in water, solids and liquid	3.5 oz.	127
Tuna, uncooked Bluefin	3.5 oz.	145
Yellowfin	3.5 oz.	133
Tuna-noodle casserole home recipe, with noodles, canned cream of mushroom soup, cheese	4 oz.	295
Tuna salad with celery, mayonnaise, pickle, onion, egg	1 c.	351
Turkey—All types, roasted flesh and skin	3.5 oz.	223
light meat	3.5 oz.	176
dark meat	3.5 oz.	203
Turkey potpie home recipe	1 piece	557
frozen, commercially prepared	1 small pie	461
Turnip greens cooked, leaves and stems	1 c.	29
canned	1 c.	26

Protein (gr.)	Fat (gr.)	Carbohydrate (gr.)		Sodium (mg)
		Total	Fiber	
28.0	.8	0	0	41
25.2	4.1	0	0	—
24.7	3.0	0	0	37
18.0	14.0	23.0	—	770
30.2	21.7	7.2	—	high to very high
31.9	9.6	0	0	—
32.9	3.9	0	0	82
30.0	8.3	0	0	99
24.4	31.7	43.4	.9	641
13.6	24.3	47.0	.7	863
3.2	.3	5.3	1.0	low
2.2	.4	4.7	1.0	345

Food	Amount	Calories
Turnip greens (cont.) frozen chopped, cooked	1 c.	38
Turnips raw	1 c.	44
boiled, drained, diced	1 c.	36
V		
Veal Chuck, braised (85% lean, 15% fat)	3.5 oz.	235
Flank, stewed (60% lean, 40% fat)	3.5 oz.	390
Foreshank, stewed (86% lean, 14% fat)	3.5 oz.	216
Loin, broiled (77% lean, 23% fat)	3.5 oz.	234
Rib, roasted (82% lean, 18% fat)	3.5 oz.	269
Round with rump, broiled (79% lean, 21% fat)	3.5 oz.	216
Vegetable juice cocktail canned	1 c.	42
Vegetables, mixed frozen, cooked	1 c.	117
Venison uncooked	3.5 oz.	126

Protein (gr.)	Fat (gr.)	Carbohydrate (gr.)		Sodium (mg)
		Total	Fiber	
4.2	.5	6.5	1.7	28
1.5	.3	9.7	1.3	72
1.3	.3	7.7	1.4	53
27.9	12.8	0	0	80 av. per 3.5 oz. of cooked meat
23.2	32.3	0	0	80 av. per 3.5 oz. of cooked meat
28.7	10.4	0	0	80 av. per 3.5 oz. of cooked meat
26.4	13.4	0	0	80 av. per 3.5 oz. of cooked meat
27.2	16.9	0	0	80 av. per 3.5 oz. of cooked meat
27.1	11.1	0	0	80 av. per 3.5 oz. of cooked meat
2.2	.2	8.8	.7	490
5.9	.6	24.6	2.2	97
21.0	4.0	0	0	—

Food	Amount	Calories
Vinegar Cider	1 tbs.	2
Distilled	1 tbs.	2

W

Food	Amount	Calories
Waffles home recipe	1 (7″ diam.)	207
frozen	1 (7″ diam.)	188
See also Pancake and waffle mixes.		
Walnuts Black	1 oz.	179
English or Persian	1 oz.	186
Water chestnuts, Chinese raw	1 oz.	23
Watercress raw, stems and leaves	1 c.	10
Watermelon	4″ x 8″ wedge	111
Weakfish broiled	3.5 oz.	208
Welsh rabbit	3.5 oz.	179

Protein (gr.)	Fat (gr.)	Carbohydrate (gr.)		Sodium (mg)
		Total	Fiber	
trace	0	.9	—	trace
—	—	.8	—	trace
6.9	7.3	27.9	.1	353
5.3c	4.6	31.2	.1	478
5.9	16.9	4.2	.5	1
4.2	18.3	4.5	.6	1
.4	.1	5.4	.2	6
1.1	.2	1.5	.4	26
2.1	.9	27.4	1.3	4
24.6	11.4	0	0	560 w/salt in water
8.1	13.6	6.3	0	332

Food	Amount	Calories
Wheat flours All-purpose or family, enriched, sifted	1 c.	422
Cake or pastry	1 c.	353
Self-rising, enriched	1 c.	444
Whole-wheat	1 c.	402
Wheat germ toasted	1 tbs.	15
Wheat products—Packaged, used mainly as hot breakfast cereals Wheat, rolled, cooked	1 c.	181
Wheat, whole meal, cooked	1 c.	111
Wheat and malted barley cereal, toasted quick-cooking	1 c.	160
instant-cooking	1 c.	197
Wheat products—Packaged, used mainly as ready-to-eat breakfast cereals Wheat, puffed, plain, added nutrients	1 c.	55
Wheat, puffed, presweetened, added nutrients	1 c.	144

Protein (gr.)	Fat (gr.)	Carbohydrate (gr.)		Sodium (mg)
		Total	Fiber	
12.2	1.2	88.3	.3	2
7.3	.8	76.9	.2	2
11.7	1.3	93.5	.5	1360
16.1	2.4	85.8	2.8	4
1.6	.4	2.1	.2	trace
5.3	1.0	40.8	1.2	713
4.4	.7	23.2	.7	523
4.9	.7	32.6	.5	178
7.4	.7	39.7	.7	252
2.3	.2	11.9	.3	1
2.3	.8	33.8	.3	62

Food	Amount	Calories
Wheat products (cont.) Wheat, shredded, plain, without added nutrients or salt	1 oblong biscuit or ½ c. spoon-size	89
Wheat flakes, added nutrients, without added salt	1 c.	107
Whipped cream. *See* Cream.		
Whipped topping canned (pressurized)	1 tbs.	10
prepared from mix	1 tbs.	10
Whitefish, lake baked, stuffed	3.5 oz.	215
smoked	3.5 oz.	155
White sauce. *See* Sauces.		
Wild rice uncooked	½ c.	329
boiled with chicken broth, salt added	½ c.	108
Wine. *See* Beverages.		

Y/Z

Yam uncooked	1 med.	101

Protein (gr.)	Fat (gr.)	Carbohydrate (gr.)		Sodium (mg)
		Total	Fiber	
2.5	.5	20.1	.6	1
3.1	.5	24.4	.5	313
trace	1.0	trace	—	2
0	1.0	1.0	—	—
15.2	14.0	5.8	—	195
20.9	7.3	0	0	—
13.1	.7	70.1	.9	7
5.0	1.0	21.0	—	355
2.1	.2	23.2	.9	low

Food	Amount	Calories
Yeast Baker's, dry, active	1 tbs.	23
Brewer's	1 tbs.	23
Yogurt Whole milk	8 oz.	142
Partially skimmed	8 oz.	114
Fruit-flavored, low fat	8 oz.	230
Zucchini. *See* **Squash, summer.**		
Zwieback	1 piece	30

Protein (gr.)	Fat (gr.)	Carbohydrate (gr.)		Sodium (mg)
		Total	Fiber	
3.0	.1	3.1	—	4
3.1	.1	3.1	.1	10
6.9	7.8	11.2	0	107
7.8	3.9	11.9	0	117
10.0	3.0	42.0	0	low to moderate
.8	.6	5.3	trace	18

HEIGHT AND WEIGHT STANDARDS

Following are weight tables by height and frame, for
people aged 25 to 59, in shoes and wearing 5 pounds
of indoor clothing for men, 3 pounds for women.

MEN

Height	Small	Medium	Large
5'2"	128–134	131–141	138–150
5'3"	130–136	133–143	140–153
5'4"	132–138	135–145	142–156
5'5"	134–140	137–148	144–160
5'6"	136–142	139–151	146–164
5'7"	138–145	142–154	149–168
5'8"	140–148	145–157	152–172
5'9"	142–151	148–160	155–176
5'10"	144–154	151–163	158–180
5'11"	146–157	154–166	161–184
6'0"	149–160	157–170	164–188
6'1"	152–164	160–174	168–192
6'2"	155–168	164–178	172–197
6'3"	158–172	167–182	176–202
6'4"	162–176	171–187	181–207

HEIGHT AND WEIGHT STANDARDS

Reprinted through the courtesy of Metropolitan Life Insurance Company.

WOMEN

Height	Small	Medium	Large
4'10"	102–111	109–121	118–131
4'11"	103–113	111–123	120–134
5'0"	104–115	113–126	122–137
5'1"	106–118	115–129	125–140
5'2"	108–121	118–132	128–143
5'3"	111–124	121–135	131–147
5'4"	114–127	124–138	134–151
5'5"	117–130	127–141	137–155
5'6"	120–133	130–144	140–159
5'7"	123–136	133–147	143–163
5'8"	126–139	136–150	146–167
5'9"	129–142	139–153	149–170
5'10"	132–145	142–156	152–173
5'11"	135–148	145–159	155–176
6'0"	138–151	148–162	158–179

Daily Food Diary

Most of us eat more than we think, and more
often. Sometimes we eat too much of one type
of food, or not enough of another, creating a

First Day

Breakfast

Lunch

Dinner

Snacks

Daily Food Diary

nutritional imbalance. Use this sample diary to
record and evaluate your food intake or to set
up your own meal plans.

Second Day

Breakfast

Lunch

Dinner

Snacks

10-Week Progress Chart for Weight Loss

Weigh yourself once a week (for example, every Monday if you begin your diet on a Monday), on the same scale, at the same time of day, wearing approximately the same amount of clothing. The first entry in the chart would come at the end of one full week of following your program.

Starting Weight_____   Goal Weight_____

Starting Date_____   Goal Date_____

	Weight	Loss
Week 1		
Week 2		
Week 3		
Week 4		
Week 5		
Week 6		
Week 7		
Week 8		
Week 9		
Week 10		

Abbreviations Used
in This Book

approx.	approximately
av.	average
c.	cup(s)
choc.	chocolate
diam.	diameter
ea.	each
fl.	fluid
gr.	gram(s)
IU	international unit
lb.	pound
lg.	large
mcg	microgram(s)
med.	medium
mg	milligram(s)
oz.	ounce(s)
pkg.	package
serv.	serving(s)
tbs.	tablespoon(s)
tsp.	teaspoon(s)
w/	with
w/o	without

Guide to Equivalent Weights and Measures

By Volume (Liquid/Fluid)

1 cup = ½ pint = 8 fluid ounces = 237 milliliters
4 cups = 1 quart = 32 fluid ounces = 0.946 liter
4 quarts = 1 gallon = 128 fluid ounces = 3.785 liters

2 tablespoons = 1 fluid ounce = 30 milliliters
16 tablespoons = 1 cup = 237 milliliters
3 teaspoons = 1 tablespoon = 15 milliliters

⅓ cup = 5 tablespoons + 1 teaspoon
¾ cup = 12 tablespoons
⅞ cup = 14 tablespoons

By Weight (Avoirdupois)

1 ounce = 28.35 grams
3½ ounces = 100 grams
1 pound = 16 ounces = 453.6 grams
1 kilogram = 1000 grams = 2.2 pounds

Commercial Canned Goods

Av. Net Weight	Approx. Cups
8 oz.	1
10½–12 oz.	1¼
14–16 oz.	1¾
16–17 oz.	2
1 lb. 4 oz. (20 oz.)	2½
1 lb. 13 oz. (29 oz.)	3½